*The Magic Zablet is a st[...]
who comes into the posse[ssion of an]
enchanted tablet computer.*

*Using this computer Millie Tyler visits
the cyber world and encounters the kind of
friends and foes, acquaintances and
tricksters and trials and tribulations that
people find each and every day on the
internet.*

*If only Millie can better realise who
really means well and what to stay away
from; then she can get home ...*

TOPICS COVERED IN THIS BOOK

Cyberbullying

Privacy

Trolls

Phishing

Geolocation

Great Offers

Messages (tweets) You Didn't Mean

Be Careful What You Say Online

Viruses

Online Pictures Causing Problems

Digital Identity and Footprint

Personal Information

Passwords

Hackers

Online "Friends" – Who Are They?

Who Can Help?

What Happens When Your Data Is Stolen?

Social Networking Sites

Trust

To Mia and Izzy,
I love reading to you so much I wrote you a book.

THE MAGIC ZABLET

James Gosnold

Millie Tyler was a girl just like any girl. Just like you in fact. Unless you are a boy of course, in which case she is a *bit* different but still probably quite like you in most ways.

Today was a fairly normal day. A normal day in Millie's house meant that Dad went to work in a huge rush, often running out of the door with a piece of toast hanging from his mouth as he shouted through crumby, buttery, clenched teeth, "Gye kidsh!" (Which roughly translates as, "Bye, kids!")

The remainder of the family, which meant Millie, her mum and her little brother, Harry, had their breakfast together.

After that Mum usually walked Millie and Harry to school unless it was cold or raining, when she would take them in the car instead, which made her feel a little guilty as she knew it was environmentally unfriendly for such a short journey.

It was only a short walk, and as it was nearly the summer holidays Millie enjoyed the walk and got to see her friends who were also on their way to school.

The sun was already shining, so it was nice and warm even though it was still early in the day.

The first friend Millie and Harry saw on the way to school that day was Theo. Theo had curly dark hair and was in Millie's class. He was nicknamed Clumsy because he often dropped things and bumped into other things.

Theo was dashing along the pavement on his fire-engine red scooter, with his mum trailing behind. When he saw Millie he was so pleased that he put an arm up to wave to her, shouting, "Mill! Mill! Mill!" while performing little jumps on his scooter which to him were of Evel Knievel proportions. (Ask your parents who he was.)

Crash! Theo didn't see the tree directly in his path, chiefly because he wasn't looking where he was going.

He didn't hurt himself too much, but the scooter looked a bit less bright red and a bit tattier.

His mum ranted at him: "THEO, I'VE TOLD YOU A THOUSAND TIMES – LOOK WHERE YOU ARE GOING!"

And that was why he was known as Clumsy. Theo was always doing things like that.

Further on, by the church which was just down the road from the school, Millie and Harry saw Nancy. Because she could be bossy at times, Millie called her Naggy Nancy. But not usually when she was in earshot.

Millie called her that more when she was talking about Nancy with Mum and Dad at home. Nancy was fiercely competitive.

Harry liked Nancy, partly because she wore funny T-shirts with characters on, but mainly because she was often naughty. He knew that that wasn't really a good reason to like someone, but he couldn't help it.

And quite often Nancy's mischief got Millie into bother.

Like the time they were supposed to paint trees in their art lesson and they painted dinosaurs instead.

Millie insisted it had been Nancy's idea because she had said, "They're green like trees so it's OK, Mrs Barker won't mind."

But Mrs Barker did mind. Detention proved that.

And then there was Ethel.

Ethel Morgan was popular at school and had a lot of friends, but she didn't like Millie. She and Millie were the tallest girls in the class and had been friends when they began at the school, but for some reason Ethel had changed her mind about Millie, which meant one thing when Ethel was around:

Trouble.

At the end of the school day Mum collected Millie and Harry and they walked home along the same route.

Theo didn't crash his scooter this time, but he did drop his schoolbag, scattering books all over the pavement outside the school, because he was chasing Nancy, who had been teasing him about his curly hair, and about being clumsy.

When Millie and Harry got home they had some tea and played in the garden. Not too long after that, Dad came home from work. He came straight out to see them.

He seemed in a very good mood and said, "Hi, kids, I'm home! Let's go out and grab a bite to eat tonight."

Millie and Harry loved going out for dinner (especially desserts) so they didn't wait about and darted upstairs to get changed.

Dad then said, "I'll be with you in just a minute, kids. I just need to check something on my computer," and off he went to sit down in front of it.

"I have a highest bid on AuctionBay for a Zablet which would be great for you; you're old enough now," he said to Millie.

A Zablet was one of the newest, latest tablet computers available to buy.

"You can play games on them, watch films, read books, learn – there are so many apps you really can do almost anything! The auction is nearly over so I can see if we've won."

They left him to it.

After ten minutes or so Mum shouted down, "Is it finished yet, dear? The children are famished, and so am I for that matter."

Dad called back, "Just another minute, dear. It's nearly finished and I think we are *still* the winning bid! Hang on, just a few more seconds … Nearly … YEEESSS! We got it! A nearly new Zablet for just twenty-five pounds! What a bargain! Both of the children will get such good use out of it!"

Dad had no idea just how right he was …

"How do we get it?" asked Mum.

"It said 'collection only', and the person selling it actually has a shop right near here, so we can pick it up on the way to dinner," said Dad.

"The username is MadamTwinkle1948 and they have a second-hand shop in Old Town. I can't say I recall it, but let's pop in on the way!"

Old Town looked glorious on this early summer's evening. The pretty old shops with their black-and-white painted fronts seemed to glow almost magically as the sky pulsated red.

There were all manner of shops, some selling old things like antiques and old-fashioned sweets, some selling new things and some were used as restaurants. Millie and her family had eaten in one of them once for Mum's birthday.

However, they walked from one end of the High Street to the other and could not see MadamTwinkle1948's shop anywhere.

"How odd," said Dad.

"Perhaps somebody was messing us about on the Internet - it does happen, you know. I've read about it. Or I could have got the address wrong. I really don't think so though."

Disappointment was etched across Millie's face.

"Never mind, Millie. Perhaps we can get you another tablet soon if Dad looks around a bit more on his computer," suggested Mum, sensing her disappointment.

"This Zablet sounded great though, Mum," said Millie.

"I've never had one before, and this one sounded amazing. Lots of my friends in school have them. I wish we could have got *this* one."

No sooner had Millie uttered that last sentence than the sky began to glow redder still and an unusual breeze began swirling around them, gentle but somehow pushing them back up the road from where they had walked towards where the car was parked.

"That breeze might make it a bit nippy. Before we know it, there could even be rain. Let's walk back to the car now and go and get some grub," decided Dad for them all.

As they trotted along Millie was reading the names of the shops out loud: "Olde Sweet Shop … Cribbin's Barbers … La Prêt à Pizza … THE TWINKLE SECOND-HAND SHOP!"

They all stopped and stared. There it was.

THE TWINKLE SECOND-HAND SHOP

It was tiny in comparison to the shops around it, but with a window jam-packed full of curiosities.

An old wooden bureau, a dusty lamp, a teddy bear that Harry was certain was following him with its eyes as he hid behind Mum and then behind Millie. The shop was almost dark inside, with twinkly lights like stars in the night sky.

"But that's impossible!" spluttered Dad."This shop wasn't here when we walked by a minute ago. It wasn't! It can't have been! We can't all have missed it, can we?!"

They shook their heads.

"Well, I never. How extraordinary. I suppose we had better go in then, hadn't we? Remarkable."

Dad went in first, Millie and Harry following behind him, with Mum bringing up the rear. Although the shop was quite dark it was also pretty inside, with very busy shelves and tables stacked with all sorts of goods of every shape and size.

Millie noticed a snow globe on one shelf, snow swirling around and above a scene of a pretty town. It was lovely, but what was strange was that the snow was floating when nobody seemed to be around to have shaken it.

Harry also noticed something odd, which was that the teddy bear in the window, the one he had noticed from outside the shop, was now facing into the shop. The bear was perfectly still, but the eyes still followed him as he walked, holding Mum's hand.

"Erm, hello? Hello, is anybody here?" shouted Dad, hoping the person selling the Zablet would hurry up and hand it over so they could get out and have their dinner quickly.

"Here? Hungry rumbling tummies is what I can hear," chimed a voice that seemed to come from above their heads.

They all looked upwards and saw a lady perched on the highest of the shelves above them.

She was holding something that glowed and illuminated her face.

"I was wondering when you would get here. I do need to get out to dinner myself, you know. And my shop can't stay here all night."

Surely she means stay *open*, not stay *here*, thought Millie.

Even up in the darkness of the vaulted ceiling they could see she was wearing a multi-coloured headscarf, big earrings and lots of loud, shiny jewellery. And then, without warning, she jumped from the shelf and almost floated down before landing right in front of them.

"Madam Twinkle. Pleased to meet you, I should think. This is yours now," she said, and thrust the Zablet firmly into Millie's hands.

How did she know it was for Millie?

"I don't have a need for it any more, as I've filled my shop with lots of other bits and bobs, as you can see. I'm sure you children are going to have a lot of fun with this."

The Tyler family were taking all of this in when suddenly Madam Twinkle roared, "TEDDY BEAR, stop being so nosey! Turn back around and look *out* of the shop, will you!"

They all looked towards the front of the shop. The teddy bear was facing out of the window, but only Harry noticed it had been facing the other way a moment ago. Nobody had been near it or touched it.

"How am I ever going to sell that bear if he insists on turning around instead of looking out of the window for shoppers to see him and his cute itty-bitty little nose?" muttered the shop lady to herself.

"Pay the lady now, darling, and let's go," said Mum, prodding Dad in the ribs.

"No need, my dear," said Madam Twinkle, brushing away Dad's hand holding the money. "I'm so happy to see this Zablet go to a good home, with children with a taste for adventure, that you can have it free of charge or obligation, as long as you promise to take good care of it. You will, won't you, Millie and Harry?"

Millie wanted to ask Madam Twinkle how she knew their names but didn't as she wanted even more to get out of this strange shop as quickly as possible.

So she just nodded.

"Well, thank you very much, Madam Twinkle. Have a lovely evening and I'm sure we'll visit your shop again soon. Byeeee!" said Dad rather unconvincingly.

As they turned to leave, Madam Twinkle put her hand on Millie's shoulder, bent forward and whispered to her, "Look after it, dear. For adventures beyond the places you dream of, to places to which you cannot travel by car or by train or by plane - to make the magic happen - put your writing hand on the screen and close your eyes for precisely ten seconds."

"Um … OK," stammered Millie, not knowing what else to say.

"Others will want it and try to trick you. Don't drop it. Don't use it after bedtime. Make your passwords impossible for anyone else to guess," continued the lady.

"Yes, all a good idea, thank you, Madam Twinkle," said Dad whilst attempting to shepherd the family out of the shop. "I'll ensure she is a worthy custodian of the Zablet."

Madam Twinkle ignored him, still looking Millie straight in the eyes. "People may not be who they say they are, and things may not be what they seem. Take care, young Millie."

And at that the Tyler family left the shop and went for their long overdue meal.

Millie and Harry were super-excited to have a new toy to play games on at home (although Dad insisted the Zablet wasn't a toy), but when they got back from dinner that night Mum was insistent. "It's very late, it's a school night. You'll have to wait until you're home tomorrow before getting your hands on the Zablet."

The following day school dragged, although Millie enjoyed telling friends (and even a half-interested teacher) about her new Zablet. Nancy was particularly fascinated, even wanting to know what colour it was and if she could come back to Millie's house after school to see it.

That was not going to happen, as Nancy's mother had other plans for her, but Millie was secretly pleased, as she wanted to use it herself when she got home.

Home time eventually came, and during the walk back past the woods Millie saw something on the floor by a tree.

Mum had spotted it too. "Oh, that's a shame, it looks as if a birdhouse has fallen down from that tree," said Mum, and Harry ran over to it.

"Don't pick it up – it might be dirty," she called after him.

Too late – Harry already had it in his hands, turning it over and inspecting it.

"It looks like the hook is broken," he diagnosed. "I bet you could fix it and we could bring it back tomorrow for the birds."

"That's a nice idea, Harry," said Mum. "Squeeze it into Millie's schoolbag, and when she does her homework later that will remind us to try and repair it."

"OK!" said Harry, excited that they had a new project at hand.

"And wash your hands!" said Mum.

Once home and out of their school uniforms, the children occupied themselves in the garden and talked about their day with Mum. Millie had been presented with a gold star in school for helping tidy up, and Harry for comforting a girl who had hurt her knee falling over. They were nice children, weren't they?

But throughout the afternoon Millie was thinking of something else. Something in the back of her mind was nagging away (and this time it wasn't Nancy).

Of course! The Zablet! How could she have forgotten?

With walking home and then the birdhouse, it had completely slipped her mind!

Millie jumped down from the dining table and ran to the cupboard in the hallway where Dad said the Zablet should be kept. And there it was.

She took it out and, being careful not to drop it, sped to the living room, flopped down on the sofa and pressed the big triangular button on the front, which was underneath the big screen. The button said HOME on it.

The Zablet made a chirping noise like a robotic sparrow as the screen illuminated and then displayed lots of brightly coloured icons.

Millie read them aloud. "Titter. InstaPic. Photos. Videos. FaceSpace."

"Millie, what are you doing? You didn't say you were going on the Zablet. Don't you want to play outside?" asked

Harry as he walked into the room and across to the sofa, wiping peanut butter from his mouth.

"Look, Harry, there are so many games and apps to play with, I hear Mum and Dad and other grown-ups talking about these all the time. I think Mum even talks to Auntie Sarah sometimes using this one, called Chatta – maybe we could try and talk to her now! Or we could play this game where you can build your own farm and have to look after the animals! Or we could take funny pictures of each other! Or we could …"

"Millie! You need to do your homework before you're allowed to play with the Zablet or anything else," said Mum, poking her head around the door of the living room.

Disappointed, Millie put down the Zablet and collected her schoolbag from the hallway.

As she was a well-behaved and clever girl Millie set about her homework, some spelling exercises which were not too difficult. She had to write a word beginning with each letter of the alphabet, in alphabetical order.

When Millie got to *F* she wrote *Feather* and then she heard a peculiar noise, like a whistle. Well, five short whistles to be exact.

She looked around, but nobody was in the room with her. Harry was with Mum in the kitchen.

Strange she thought.

When Millie got to *R* she wrote *Raspberry* in her exercise book, which was the longest word she had used so far and was quite pleased with it, especially as she was certain she had spelled it correctly.

And then she heard the whistling sound again. Where was it coming from?

She walked to the living-room door but could hear Harry and Mum were still in the kitchen, so it definitely wasn't them. Nobody else was in the house.

Millie sat back down and carried on with the task at hand. For a word beginning with *S* she wrote *Spaceman*, for *T* she wrote *Tickle*, *U* got *Under*, for *V* it was *Vanish*, *W* was *Wonderful*, *X* was tricky but after a little thought she wrote *X-ray*, *Y* was *Yellow*, and then she stopped on *Z*.

"Hmmm, *Z* – what's a good word beginning with *Z*?" she wondered out loud.

And then Millie heard the whistles again, only this time she knew precisely where they came from and she looked down at what was lying next to her on the sofa … *Z* was for *Zablet*!

Millie picked up the Zablet and turned it on. She swiped through the screens, looking at some of the games and apps, but every time she lingered the Zablet whistled, as if wanting her to choose something else.

Harry came in and sat next to Millie.

"Watcha doing, Millie? What game are you going to play?" he said, eyeing the Zablet.

"Don't know," replied Millie. "It keeps whistling. Do you think it's broken?"

"Maybe that was why the funny lady wanted to get rid of it," said Harry. "Or maybe it wants you to do what the funny lady said. Put your hand on it and close your eyes."

"I think," said Millie, "that lady was a bit silly. I think she was just trying to be all mysterious or scary or tease me."

"Well, I'm putting the TV on. Mum said we could watch it for a while until dinner," and Harry picked up the remote control, turned the TV on and changed the channel to LittleOdeon.

"*Monkey and Duds* is on," he chirped. "Excellent!"

Harry was very quickly absorbed in his favourite cartoon show. *Monkey and Duds* was a cartoon about, well, a monkey who pretends to be a human child and goes to school with other real children.

"Duds" was the only word he could say, so that was the Monkey's name in the real children's school. The fact he was really a monkey made matters difficult and he often got into scrapes, but always managed to keep the secret.

Millie looked back at the Zablet and decided to give what Madam Twinkle had said a go, because having a Zablet that was actually magic would be pretty cool. She *had* to find out if it was.

Millie's writing hand was her right hand, so she placed it flat on the screen, closed her eyes and began counting. One … two … three … four … five … six … seven … eight … nine … TEN …

Millie wasn't sure when exactly she was supposed to open her eyes, but the Zablet whistled again so she did, and what a surprise she got!

Harry wasn't sitting next to her. Millie wasn't on a sofa.

She wasn't even in the living room any longer.

And she wasn't holding the Zablet, just clutching her schoolbag, which had been on her lap.

Millie was sitting on a log in what seemed to be a forest.

It was quite dark because there were trees everywhere, making a sort of roof. And it wasn't really scary, because it was daytime and sunlight was streaming through the gaps in the trees.

And it was oh so noisy!

Birdsong and chattering voices everywhere, coming from all around. Left, right, behind, in front and above.

"Hello!" said a voice directly behind her, louder than the others.

Millie turned around and was surprised to see a small man with wild scruffy orange hair sticking out from under his green cap.

"Are you following me?" he asked.

"Um, no …" said Millie.

"Oh. Am I following you then?" asked the little man.

"No!" said Millie thinking that was a strange question. "I don't know you at all and I don't know where I am either. Where is this?"

"OK, I can help you with that. I'm Crackers and *this* is Titter!" he replied with a beaming smile and outstretched arms. "Are you *sure* I'm not following you?" he went on. "I can hear you tweeting."

"I'm not following you, and you're not following me!" said Millie, a little more impatiently. She was starting to get upset and she demanded, "WHERE AM I AND HOW DID I GET HERE?!"

"Ooh, that will get you more followers," said Crackers. "You know, SHOUTING like that. Just you wait and see. I think I *will* follow you; you're interesting. I like you."

"Leave me alone," said Millie, and she stormed off in a direction she hoped would take her to the edge of the forest and the way home.

"Hey, Millie, wait up!" pleaded Crackers, his little legs moving as quickly as they would take him.

Millie stopped and glared at him. "HOW do you know my name?" she blared. "I didn't tell you my name."

"I'm following you now, Millie," explained Crackers breathlessly, resting against the nearest tree. "So I know lots about you! That's how it works in Titter! Everybody and everything can hear what you say. Go on, give it another go and you'll see what I mean!"

"I hate this stupid forest and I want to go home," said Millie as loudly as she could without actually shouting.

Crackers stood back up straight and a look of worry set across his face. "Uh-oh! Now you've done it."

A bluebird fluttered down from the tree Crackers had been leaning against, hovered in front of Millie and tweeted at her, "I don't hate it. It's nice here. Why don't YOU go away? You're STUPID!"

Before Millie could answer that, another bird appeared and chirped, "Yes, it's nice here. YOU go away, STUPID!"

And more voices behind her said in unison, "Yes, it's nice here. YOU go away!"

A small rabbit hopped out from behind a log and stood next to Crackers. "Ooohhh, reeepeat, YOU go away, Millie!"

Faster than Millie could count, more bluebirds, rabbits, squirrels, badgers, moles and toads appeared from behind logs, trees and bushes, some shouting and some squeaking.

"Millie, YOU go away!"

The noise got louder and louder rising in a crescendo. Millie couldn't tell what was being said or who was saying it.

She suddenly felt very frightened and wanted to get away, but she was surrounded by animals, and even if she did run, she didn't know where to run to.

"STOP!" shouted one voice, louder than the others.

Millie turned to see Crackers standing in front of the forest animals holding a huge bright blue megaphone.

"Millie is new to Titter and doesn't know how it works," he announced to them all. "I think the WOW Wizard who lives by the thousand-year tree is about to say something clever. Go and listen there, won't you?"

A few birds fluttered their wings and flew away towards the centre of the forest, followed by rabbits hopping off after them. The squirrels ran back up the trees and other animals began to scamper off.

Millie sat on the ground with her head in her hands, weeping. Crackers sat down next to her.

"What just happened, Crackers?" she sobbed.

"This is the strangest and most horrible forest I've ever been to. The animals shout at you, I don't understand how I got here and I don't know how to get back. I'm stuck and I'm scared."

Crackers nudged nearer and spoke gently. "You're in Titter-land, Millie. That's how it works here. You have to be really careful what you say."

He put his hand gently on her shoulder and continued. "If you say something loudly enough, everybody in Titter can hear it. Not everybody understands it or knows why you said it, or why you were angry; they just know *what* you said. And then they tweet to everyone else they know. And there are some bad-tempered people in this forest, like the WOW Wizard. You don't want him to know what you said."

Millie asked, "What does *WOW Wizard* mean, Crackers? I mean the *WOW* bit, I think I know what a wizard is, although I've never met one."

"*WOW* is an acronym, Millie. Short for *Wicked or Wise*. Sometimes he's wicked, sometimes he's wise," explained Crackers. "So the WOW Wizard can be bad or he can be helpful, but he's the biggest cheese in these parts, and also the only one who can help you get back home, because he's been around here the longest."

Millie thought for a moment. "But this isn't real, is it? I mean this is just in the Zablet, isn't it? It's like a dream or a game. I can go home whenever I want, can't I?"

Crackers replied, "When the Titter Birds and forest animals called you stupid, that upset you, didn't it?"

Millie nodded. Yes, it had.

Crackers walked over to the nearest tree, climbed up to the first branch and sat on it. He really was a fidget.

"If I call you ugly and silly does that make you feel sad, Millie?" said Crackers, who really did ask a lot of questions.

Millie thought about it and nodded again.

Crackers took off his green cap and scratched his curly hair, wrinkling up his face. "Pesky forest midges making my head itch," he grumbled. "If it makes you have those feelings –

sad, upset, angry or anything else – then this world *is* real, Millie, which means you *are* stuck here and we need to go and ask the WOW Wizard how we can get you back home. Let's go!"

Millie and Crackers walked for a while until they came upon a sign nailed to the trunk of a tree. It read:

HERE THE WOW WIZARD GAVE HIS 1000TH TWEET.

"We're going the right way," said Crackers, and carried on down a path between two stands of trees. Millie scampered along behind.

Before long they came to a clearing with a log lying on the ground. On it was carved:

HERE THE WOW WIZARD GAVE HIS 5000TH TWEET.

"Great!" said Crackers. "We're getting nearer to his latest tweet now."

Millie didn't really understand what was going on. She sprinted ahead of Crackers and then stopped in front of him to block his way. "Crackers! What do all these signs mean?"

Crackers stopped. "The WOW Wizard is like everyone else in Titter, Millie, except he has more followers than anyone else, which makes him more powerful than anyone else. *Everyone* hears what he says when he tweets because he is the loudest. If we can persuade him to tweet out that you should be forgiven for your angry tweet, then the others might help you."

They carried on and eventually reached a clearing in the forest with a small cottage in the middle. Pink smoke billowed from the chimney and a large group of forest-dwellers were gathered outside the door, chattering among themselves. They all looked very excited about something.

Crackers spotted a large grey owl who was in conversation with a squirrel. They were sitting on a branch together, watching the cottage for any sign of activity and then watching Millie and Crackers approach.

"Hi, Zoree!" announced Crackers.

"Why, helloooo and too-wit-too-woo to you, Crackers," responded the owl. "Long time no tweet! You've been very quiet lately."

"What's going on?" asked Crackers.

"The WOW Wizard is about to say something very important," said Zoree.

"We want to be the first to hear it. Maybe even retweet it if it's good."

Suddenly the smoke spewing from the chimney changed to yellow, then green, then red, before a shower of sparks flew up into the air followed by a sharp *bang* and a bit of a splutter, like a firework that wasn't working properly.

The cottage door creaked open and from within the dark interior strode what was most definitely a wizard. He fitted almost every wizard description ever written.

Wearing a long flowing blue robe covered with yellow stars and moon shapes, a long wispy beard that went all the way down to his red shoes and a pointy hat, he ticked most of the wizard boxes apart from the fact his beard was dark, not silver.

He was also younger than your average wizard.

The WOW Wizard marched forward to address the crowd, thrusting his staff into the air.

"To all the forest-dwellers I say, there are trolls among us," he announced.

"Wicked trolls. Hideous trolls. *Baaadd* trolls. Trolls that speak untruths about us. Trolls that seek to upset us. The trolls

22

make the forest a poisonous place, and therefore I seek your help. We must root them out and banish them before their maliciousness spoils it for everyone!"

Zoree raised a wing so he could ask a question. "WOW Wizard, I haven't seen any trolls. How can you be sure?"

"The trolls are cunning, Zoree. Devious. They use magic to disguise themselves as normal forest-dwellers," said the WOW Wizard.

"You can't tell them apart just by looking at them."

Zoree nodded and said to the others, "That's why he has more followers than me – he knows stuff."

"The WOW Wizard doesn't seem very wicked, or wise really," whispered Millie to Crackers. "He hasn't done anything wicked and doesn't even know how to tell who the trolls are."

"He has bad days, Millie," said Crackers "The wizard wears a red robe when he's wicked."

Millie thought this land was very strange and unpredictable indeed and wanted to get home more than ever.

Suddenly a commotion broke out behind them and the friends saw a rabbit who was bigger than all the others bouncing around wildly and jumping on the heads of the other forest dwellers, shouting things like, "All silly! All stinky! All stooopid! LOL!"

Everyone backed away from the big rabbit as he carried on shouting rude things before finally yelling, "TROLLS, take the WOW Wizard's cottage!"

Before their eyes a squirrel grew to ten times its normal size and a Titter Bird snapped the branch it was sitting on because it had grown so big and heavy. It landed with a bump in front of them. The newly large squirrel and bird both shed their disguises to reveal themselves as knobbly, gnarly, warty trolls and they ran into the WOW Wizard's cottage, slamming shut the door.

The WOW Wizard hastily pulled a wand from his robe and began to conjure a spell which was supposed to open the door. But as he chanted the magic words the trolls shouted ever louder and the WOW Wizard couldn't get the words out.

He tried to bellow his magic words louder, but every time the trolls raised the volume even more. Among the forest dwellers there was more than one troll joining in.

Millie looked frantically around. She really needed the WOW Wizard to help her get home, but he couldn't right now, and he was getting more and more frantic and stressed at being locked out of his cottage.

"Mr WOW Wizard, I have an idea how to work out who the trolls are," Millie shouted above the commotion made by shouting trolls and an enraged wizard.

The wizard stopped waving his arms in the air and shouting at the door of his cottage and turned to see who had spoken.

Then, glaring at Millie, the WOW Wizard poked his wand at her and said, "Titter ye not! You're just a silly, annoying little girl! That's what the forest animals all said! I heard them!"

As he spoke and poked at Millie his face seemed to get redder and angrier, and at the same time his robe, it was turning red.

"And you said bad things about the Titter forest. TERRIBLE things!" he ranted.

"I … I … didn't mean it," was all Millie could say in response.

"Aaahhh, but you SAID it, young lady. YOU said it. We all heard. It was retweeted many, many times."

"Millie! Tell him your idea now! Before he turns completely wicked, or you won't be getting back home for goodness knows how long," urged Crackers.

Millie clenched her fists, her own face getting quite red, and said, "DON'T. YOU. TALK. TO. ME. LIKE .THAT!"

The WOW Wizard stopped ranting for a moment and Millie took her chance and carried on.

"I'm not a silly little girl. I'm here by accident from the real world, somehow by using a magic Zablet. I got upset and I said something I didn't mean, or at least didn't know about, but just one forest animal heard me and retweeted what I'd said. Before I knew it the whole forest was repeating it and everyone was angry with me."

The WOW Wizard lowered his wand-pointing arm and his robe seemed to be slowly turning a softer purple and then back to blue. His face was less red and he was not so much glaring at Millie but more just observing her now, in, well, quite a wise and knowing way.

"And I do know how to tell who the trolls are!" repeated Millie before the WOW Wizard spoke again.

The wizard spoke more gently than before. "What is your name, little girl?"

Millie told him.

"And a magic Zablet, you say? Well, Millie," said the WOW Wizard, "first of all, my apologies for turning so red; I have terrible indigestion. I am aware that things can, shall we say, get out of hand in the wonderful world of Titter."

He pointed at the animals gathered outside his cottage (which now had trolls looking out of the windows and laughing at them).

"These friends are prone to echoing one's words, broadcasting those words out to people and places where the person who said it might not have wanted them heard. You must consider more what you are saying. That is the number-one rule of Titter!"

He continued, "Now, please tell me how I can identify which of the animals are actually trolls in disguise so I can delete them one by one with a spell. My magic isn't powerful enough to delete them all in one go, and without your help I could delete innocent forest dwellers in error, you see.

"If you can help me, I will soon get you back home," he added.

Millie was excited now and explained her idea. "OK. Trolls can never say anything nice. All they do is say horrible things to upset people. Nobody knows why, but some creatures just act like that – especially in this land, it seems. If we talk to the forest animals one by one and say something nice to them, only the trolls will be horrid in reply and you can delete them!"

Crackers jumped up and down, clapping his hands. "Great idea, Mills! I love it! Big favourite!"

Millie thought Crackers did have some strange sayings, which now apparently included calling her Mills.

"Well, it does sound as if your idea has some merit, Millie," responded the WOW Wizard after a moment's thought.

"Let's go for a walk, shall we? I thought I heard some of the shouting from over there." He pointed towards a cluster gathered by a tree.

The first creature they approached was a toad. A very big toad, standing on his two hind legs and wearing a tweed jacket and a flat cap, but a toad nonetheless.

The toad looked at them with his big eyes as they approached.

"Oh no, it's the WOW Wizard. what do you want? I ain't done nothing wrong! Nothing, I tell ya!"

"We shall be the judge of that," said the wizard, and turned to Millie.

"Go on, Millie," he said. "You test him."

Millie thought for a moment, while the toad stared at her with his big eyes.

"Mr Toad, your jacket is lovely, and I must say you look quite dapper with the matching hat."

The toad, who was shaking a little and clearly quite nervous, suddenly smiled. "Well, thank you, young lady. You are very nice to say so. Have a great day!" and off he walked.

"He isn't one," said Millie to the WOW Wizard and Crackers. "Let's try another."

The next candidate was a blue bird, flapping around above the others.

"Hello I'm a Titter Bird," she said as they approached.

"Well, hello, Titter Bird," said Millie. "You are very pretty and have a lovely coat of blue feathers."

"Oooohhh, thank you ever so much. I'm going to tell everyone you said that!" tweeted the bird. "I really like your dress too!" And off she flapped to a branch high up above them.

Millie was beginning to doubt her idea. What if the trolls were clever enough to *pretend* to be nice when they were being tested?

Next they approached a pink rabbit, who was at the back of the group, seemingly trying to hop away.

"Hey, Miss Rabbit, I have something to tell you. Can you stop a minute?" asked Millie.

The rabbit somewhat reluctantly hopped back towards them.

Millie then said, "Miss Rabbit, I love your floppy ears and your fluffy pink fur. You are just the cutest thing!"

The rabbit twitched her nose, looked around a little shiftily and then back at them and said, "Well, I don't like you. Nobody likes you. Nobody likes them either.' She pointed at the WOW Wizard and Crackers. 'They're stupid!"

Millie looked at the wizard. "Mr WOW Wizard, I do believe we've got one."

The WOW Wizard nodded at Millie and then strode forward until he towered above the rather scared-looking rabbit. He raised his wand above his head and said these words:

You don't care how you make others feel,
But this spell will reveal the truth whole.
Stay in the forest if you are real,
Vanish to dust IF YOU ARE A TROLL!

A little pop and a puff of smoke and the pink rabbit disappeared before their eyes, leaving just a small pile of smouldering cinders where she had been standing.

"Have you killed her?" asked Millie.

"Oh no, not at all," chuckled the WOW Wizard. "I've just deleted a troll from Titter where it wasn't welcome and banished it back to its own land."

Zoree, who had crept up right next to the WOW Wizard, excitedly clapped his wings together and jumped up and down, shouting, "Let's find another troll, WOW Wizard. That was awesome!"

And so off they went in search of another troll to delete.

Soon they saw a pretty little furry bear picking flowers and smelling them in a luscious-looking glade. *Surely* this beautiful cuddly creature couldn't be a troll in disguise?

The WOW Wizard strode forward and said, "I say, young bear."

The bear looked round, sneezed and said, "Oh, I'm sorry, I love buttercups, but they make me sneeze oodles. Hi, how are you?"

"Why, I'm quite well, bear, and thank you for asking," said the WOW Wizard, and then whispered to the others, "Clearly this bear is in no way a troll. She seems very polite and is unBEARably cute. Definitely no troll to see here. Let's go."

"You have to do the test," said Crackers. "We have to be sure about this."

The WOW Wizard studied the bear, then looked reluctantly back at Crackers, adjusted his hat, fiddled nervously with his wand, then back at the bear again.

"Ahem, OK, if you insist. I suppose I should," he agreed.

"Well then, young bear, I have something I would like to say to you. And erm … um … it is this. I very much like this glade in which you have chosen to view and enjoy flowers – what excellent taste you have."

The cute bear smiled slightly and replied, "Thank you, WOW Wizard. Thank you very much. But you see, it isn't a glade. IT'S A PIXIE GARDEN and YOU'RE AN IDIOT for not knowing the difference!" By now she was gnashing her teeth.

Quickly she cupped her hand over her mouth and looked surprised.

"Whoops," she said. "I think you've rumbled me."

The others looked on as the WOW Wizard once again raised his wand above his target and recited the banishment spell, as the bear vanished, leaving only a small pile of dust where she had been.

"Your stick is awesome, Mr WOW Wizard," said Crackers.

Millie giggled as she saw the WOW Wizard go red again.

"STICK? STICK?! It's a wand, you silly little man! A powerful magic WOW Wizard's wand at that!"

Millie piped up. "You should be careful calling people silly like that, Mr WOW Wizard. We might think you're a troll!"

"Hmmph …" replied the WOW Wizard. "Let's find some more."

And off they went, testing each forest animal they came across.

Millie, the WOW Wizard, Crackers and Zoree took turns saying something nice and waiting for the answer. Each time the response made it obvious who was a troll and who wasn't.

After a time they figured out it was quicker for the WOW Wizard to concentrate on spells while the other three did the talking and the test (and the WOW Wizard wasn't very good at the testing part anyway).

Before long they had banished three rabbits, three toads, two badgers, two Titter Birds, a squirrel, a bear and a flower.

Yes, that's right, a flower. Millie had said something nice to a skunk, and the flower next to them (which it turned out was a troll in disguise) started shouting all manner of horrible things to them!

"Just the trolls in my cottage to rid Titter of now," said the WOW Wizard, and led the group back to his abode. It was now eerily quiet there.

Crackers peered through one of the windows.

"Umm, WOW Wizard, I think they've run away. There's nobody inside," he said.

32

They went round to the back of the cottage and found the back door open, with troll footprints leading away – they had escaped!

The WOW Wizard looked concerned. "My, this is troubling. The remaining trolls have gone back into the forest and will be in hiding now. But before long they will be back being spiteful to others. We must continue to be vigilant."

Crackers coughed to get the WOW Wizard's attention. "Erm … Mr WOW Wizard, as Millie helped you spot the trolls, will you help her get home now?" he asked. "You did make a promise."

"Indeed I did and indeed I will," replied the WOW Wizard.

He took off his pointy blue hat and held it out to Millie. "Millie, thank you for your help, and I'm sure I don't know what we would have done without it. The magic spell to get you home requires you to leave something behind that you brought with you, something that will help the inhabitants of this world. Put it in the hat, please. Hurry along."

Millie thought for a moment. She still had her schoolbag, but didn't want to leave that as she'd need it when she returned home. She opened the bag and rummaged her fingers found something that rattled when she shook it.

Millie pulled the object out – the birdhouse!

"Will this do, wizard?" she asked.

"Of course, of course, put it in, young lady. The Titter Birds will love it. I don't believe we've ever had one of these in the forest," said the WOW Wizard, and then added a handful of grass from the floor.

Something from here,

Something from you,
Send the real girl home,
Before I count to ...
POOF!!!

Crackers, Zoree and the WOW Wizard were left standing outside the cottage, with not a single trace of Millie but for the birdhouse she had left behind.

"I never get to finish counting with that spell – it always worries me they might not get to the right place," mused the WOW Wizard.

"Still. At least there is no pile of cinders ..."

Harry was sitting on the sofa watching *Monkey and Duds*, slightly wondering where Millie was but mainly enjoying the show when a sudden popping noise made him jump and then look to his left.

There, next to him on the sofa, was Millie with the Zablet in her hands.

"Where have you been, Millie?" he asked.

"How long have I *not* been here, Harry?" she replied.

"Err, dunno, five or ten minutes? Not really sure," said Harry. (He couldn't tell the time yet.)

Millie couldn't believe that the adventure she had just been on had lasted less time than the television programme.

"I've been on an incredible adventure with the Zablet, Harry. Do you want to come next time?" asked Millie.

"Sure, sounds good," replied Harry, and popped another raisin in his mouth, wondering what on earth Millie was talking about.

Millie couldn't think of anything else for days.

Would she go on an adventure like that with the Zablet *every* time she closed her eyes and counted to ten? Could Harry or anyone else go with her?

About a week had passed when one afternoon Millie was in class sitting next to Nancy. Their form teacher, Mrs Barker, was asking the children ("Now that the summer holidays are nearly upon us …") one by one to stand up and tell the class the best or most exciting thing they had done during the school year.

Millie leaned to her left and whispered to Nancy that she had been to an enchanted forest and met a real wizard, all inside her new Zablet.

"Errr … OK, Millie … sounds like fun, but I don't think anyone is going to believe it," Nancy whispered back Nancy.

"Well," said Millie, "that's the thing. I—" The girls were abruptly interrupted as Mrs Barker boomed, "Millie Tyler! Please share your secret with the rest of the class if you aren't able to take the time to listen to others!"

Millie went red; she wasn't really about to tell the rest of the class about her adventure with an enchanted Zablet. They wouldn't believe her and might even make fun of her.

"OK, Millie, if the cat has got your tongue, perhaps *Nancy* would care to share with us what was so important that you were unable to participate in the class discussion?"

Since getting into trouble over the green dino-tree incident, Nancy had been trying extra hard to behave in school and do precisely what Mrs Barker and any other teachers told her.

She looked at Millie and then back at the glaring Mrs Barker. Then back at Millie again.

"Well?" said Mrs Barker. "We are all waiting."

Nancy mouthed, "Sorry, Millie," and stood up.

"Mrs Barker, erm … Millie just was … erm … telling me … erm … that the other day she went to an enchanted forest. Just for a few minutes."

There was a deafening silence as the rest of class stared open-mouthed at Nancy, and then Mrs Barker, and then in disbelief at Millie.

Finally the silence was shattered by the one noise Millie feared the most.

A wicked cackle of a laugh boomed from the front of the classroom.

"Ha! Ha! Haaaaaa! Ha! Ha!" cut through the quietness like a knife and sounded to Millie's ears like the most hideous noise she had ever heard.

It was Ethel Morgan, and she and Millie did not get on very well. They had been at each other's throats ever since the first day of this school term, or, more to the point, Ethel had been at Millie's throat. Ethel had a group of friends who could all be spiteful at times, and Millie and her friends often felt the brunt of that.

To be clear, Ethel was a bully.

"Millie Tyler was making up pretend stories about magic adventures! How utterly ridiculous and childish! Everybody laugh at her right now!" commanded Ethel.

And the class mostly did, apart from Millie's best friends, Theo and Nancy. Mrs Barker had to shout quite loudly over the laughter to restore order.

"Quiet, children! Millie, you will stay behind after class as a punishment for disrupting the class, especially with tales that are complete nonsense!" she admonished.

"Really, Millie Tyler, I expected better from you."

Millie hung her head and muttered, "Sorry, Mrs Barker."

She knew there was no point in arguing about it, and she didn't want her secret out in the open, but she did know Ethel had made the situation a whole lot worse for her, and when class finished Ethel smirked as she walked past Millie's desk. She had certainly enjoyed watching Millie get into trouble.

When Millie left the classroom after the ten-minute detention which had cut into her playtime, Ethel was waiting in the cloakroom with her bunch of friends.

"Hi, Millie," said Ethel as she approached. Unusually for her, she was smiling.

"I was just waiting for you to say sorry and that I feel really bad about what happened in class there. I didn't mean for you to get into so much trouble."

She held out a hand and said, "Friends?"

Now Millie would much rather be someone's friend than enemy, so she held out her hand too, but as she did so Ethel sharply withdrew hers and poked Millie in the arm.

"As if I would want to be friends with someone who makes up childish stories? Grow up!" she sneered and walked off.

Millie tried not to let it show that Ethel was upsetting her by being so nasty and she turned round to pick up her schoolbag, but it wasn't where she had left it on a bench.

She heard giggling and ran to the door that led out to the playground, where she saw two of Ethel's gang at the top of climbing frame, hanging her bag there. They all knew Millie didn't like climbing or heights and they wriggled down and ran off.

As the tears began to well up, Theo came over. "Don't worry, Millie, I'll climb up and get it back for you. Ethel's bunch of skunks are getting worse."

Now Theo might be clumsy, but he *was* good at climbing, which was fortunate because the top of a climbing frame was not the best place to be clumsy.

He shot up and back down like Spider-Man.

"Here you go, Millie. Just try and ignore them and hope they go and find someone else to bother."

"When Ethel and her gang carry on like this, I just want to go and hide," said Millie.

"Well, only one more lesson before home time – you can hide there. Come on. Let's go and find Nancy," replied Theo, dashing off.

After school Millie had to explain to Mum what had happened. (Well, she told her about being caught talking, but not about Ethel or the Zablet adventures. Millie didn't think her mum was quite ready for that – and she didn't want to worry her about Ethel's bullying so she kept it to herself.)

Millie and Harry had a playhouse at the end of the garden that Dad had built them last year. It had taken him ages to do it and he had always seemed to be cross while he was building it, but then insisted he really had enjoyed the whole process.

That holiday was to the Greek island of Mesalonia, and they had a fantastic time there doing all the usual holiday things: swimming, playing on the beach, eating ice cream and visiting idyllic little villages and interesting old towns.

The low point of the holiday had been Millie losing her toy rabbit on the beach. She had had the toy rabbit since she was a toddler and was very fond of it.

When she got home from school Millie decided to go out to the playhouse to see if she could start another Zablet adventure, out of sight of Mum and Dad.

This time she thought she would try while browsing the photos from their holiday that Mum and Dad had put on it.

Millie and Harry had loved that holiday. Could they possibly go on an adventure *there* using the Zablet?

Millie took Harry's arm and whispered, "You know I told you about my Zablet adventure? In the Titter forest? You did believe me, didn't you, Harry?"

Harry nodded but didn't say anything. He wasn't sure whether or not he believed Millie, but it sounded like a fun game.

"Let's go and play in the playhouse then," she said.

It was only a small playhouse, with room for four or five children sitting down, and all the toys and dolls in there made for even less room.

Millie laid the Zablet flat on the floor and swiped through past games and apps until they got to an icon of a palm tree which was labelled "Holiday Photos".

Millie tapped on that, which brought up other icons named after holidays they had been on, such as Spain, Gorton Regis, Great Barmow and of course Mesalonia.

Millie tapped her finger on Mesalonia and the first picture displayed was of her and Harry in the hotel swimming pool, Harry with his bright yellow Monkey and Duds branded inflatable armbands.

"That was a funny day, Millie," chuckled Harry.

"Yes, I remember," replied Millie.

"You dropped an ice cream in the swimming pool and then jumped in after it, thinking you could get it back and still eat it!"

They both laughed at that. Harry had been a bit younger then. He hadn't found it so funny at the time, but had cheered up when Millie had shared her ice cream with him.

After some more hotel swimming-pool pictures they arrived at a set of snaps taken on a day out at the beach, Millie wearing a swimming costume that was pink with white polka dots and Harry in (yes, you guessed it) yellow Monkey and Duds branded swimming shorts.

"Let's try and go back there, Harry," decided Millie. "Hold my hand and close your eyes."

Harry did what he was told, and Millie held his hand with her left hand and placed her right hand on the Zablet, checked to make sure Harry's eyes were still closed (they were) and then closed her own and began counting: One … two … three … four … five … six … seven … eight … nine … 10 …

The first sensation Millie noticed before she had even opened her eyes was that her feet felt different.

She was standing on sand and felt it scratching between her toes.

Then Millie heard Harry shouting, "Aaarrrgghhhh! Aaaarrgghhh! My feet are wet!" and opened her eyes to see him splashing around in water.

They were at the beach!

Not only that, but she recognised this beach. It was on Mesalonia, and was just how she remembered it, with the lovely white sand and shimmering blue sea.

Harry had already sat down and started building a sandcastle with his hands.

"This is amazing, Millie, it's lovely being back here. I don't know how you did it, but thank you so much for bringing me here!"

Before Millie had a chance to answer they heard a voice crying out, a whimpering, high-pitched voice.

"Heeeelllppp! Heeeellllpppp!! Pleeeeaasssse!!! Heeellllppp!!!!"

The children looked all around the beach, behind rocks, under trees, but couldn't locate the source of the voice, at least not until they looked out to sea.

And there out on a rock they could see something small, with floppy ears, waving at them and shouting even more.

"Heeeelllpppp!!!!!"

"I can't see who or what that is waving at us," said Millie.

Whatever it was seemed to be distressed, and Millie and Harry set off together along the beach to look for a boat or a raft or something that might help them sail out to rescue the trapped creature.

As they neared a cluster of rocks they heard a clicking noise, which when they listened more closely they realised was tapping out a rhythm, and then a gravelly voice singing:

I'm Sammy the Crab and I'm baaaad,
Sammy the Crab make 'em saaaad,
I took her bunny,
It was so funny,
I'm Sammy the Crab and I'm glaaaad.

Millie and Harry looked behind the rock and found the musician-cum-singer. It was an orange crab wearing big blue-rimmed glasses, splashing about in a rock pool and looking pleased with himself.

44

Harry stamped his foot in the pool to announce their presence, but when the crab saw them he jumped up in the air in fright and scuttled away behind another rock.

"We need to speak to you, Sammy," said Harry.

"Me? Why?" came a trembling voice from behind the rock.

"We heard you singing about what you did, which was mean. AND we need to borrow your glasses to see what exactly is stuck out there on that rock."

"Oooohhh, not my glasses! Love my glasses! Not lending them to you," replied Sammy, still behind the rock.

"Well, they don't look like your glasses – they are too big for you for a start," said Millie, although she felt silly talking to a rock.

"I think you stole them like you took the bunny. Give them to me now or … or … or … we'll put a big rock in your pool and ruin it!"

There was silence. Then a rustling noise. Then finally the glasses flew out from the rock and landed by their feet.

Millie put them on and looked back out at sea at the figure waving frantically from the rock, squinting so she could see more clearly (as the glasses weren't a great deal of help really).

And then she recognised who it was. It was her own toy rabbit that she had lost on holiday, and it was stuck on the rock, looking very scared!

"Sammy!" exclaimed Millie. "Get out here NOW and explain this, or your pool gets it and you won't get your glasses back!"

They listened carefully for any sign of the crab. After a short silence they heard a scuttling noise and the crab peered out.

"Errr. I'm Sammy the Crab," he said. "I'm a crab."

"Yes, we know," said Millie impatiently. "Why is my cuddly toy rabbit stuck out at sea, Sammy?"

"Oh, eeerrr … don't know. I'm a crab," he replied, looking around nervously.

"You do know!" shouted Harry. "We heard you singing about how you took it. We heard you!"

"Oh, errr, that's me rumbled then. Bang to rights. Are you going to call the police?" asked Sammy.

"Not if you tell us what happened right *now*," said Millie, poking a finger at the crabby suspect.

"Oh, errr, well, let me see. I'm a crab. Did I mention that? Probably. Well, I saw you and little Mr Yellow Shorts playing on the beach one day, and you left the bunny on a towel. I thought it looked useful, as a blanket or a pillow or a decoration for the rock pool or even a companion to keep me company. So I crabbed over and nabbed it with my claws when nobody was looking. Easiest job I've ever done, to be honest."

"So how did it get stuck out on a rock at sea, Sammy?" asked Millie.

"Yeah, I thought you would ask that next," he replied.

"Oh, errr …" (Sammy seemed to say this whenever he was nervous.)

"I took your bunny out to sea, for a swim, show it around, you know and the baddest shark in these waters swam right up to us, said he was very hungry and he fancied crab baguette for lunch." Sammy looked down (as much as a crab can actually look down) at his claws in shame.

"Oh, eeerr, well, I said to the baddest shark, 'Take the bunny, take this. Tastes lovely, much better than a crusty old crab and very nutritious for sharks, I'm told.'"

Then Sammy told them how the shark swam off with the bunny between his teeth while he made his getaway back to shore.

The shark was about to chomp down when he realised it was just fluffy fur and the crab had tricked him, so he spat it out! The bunny drifted onto the rock (it couldn't swim but floated very well) and then clambered up.

"And there it's been since yesterday," said Sammy.

Millie and Harry looked at each other. How were they going to get her bunny back? They walked out to the furthest point of rocks on the beach to get a better view. Millie was improving all the time at swimming, but it looked too dangerous to try to swim that far.

At that moment they saw a large shape swimming towards the beach, in their direction.

"Oh, eeerr, it's the shark, come back to get me!" cried Sammy – Millie and Harry hadn't realised he was behind them – and he scuttled off to hide behind another rock.

The children watched nervously as the large object swam closer. It was dark, almost round and bobbing up and down in the waves. It certainly didn't look like a shark or swim as fast as one.

As it got closer they could see two big flippers gently steering the creature in their direction.

"That's not a shark," said Harry. "We've been looking at sea animals in school, and that is a turtle."

They watched with gaping mouths as a huge turtle landed on the beach next to them.

"Hello," it said, dripping as it shuffled along. "Have you seen my eggs? I buried them here earlier and can't remember where exactly I."

The turtle looked very worried and carried on along the beach, looking here and there.

"Mrs Turtle, I'm really good at finding things, I'll help," shouted Harry, and jumped off the rock and ran after her.

"Do you remember where you were on the beach earlier?" he asked as he ran, with Millie trying to catch up.

"No, I don't. It's such a big long beach and I'm not sure I remember where exactly I was before," she replied forlornly. She was so sad she started weeping.

"Oh, errr, I got an idea," said a voice, and the children turned around to see Sammy scuttling behind them.

"Turtle flipper prints are easy to spot, and Mrs Turtle is such a big specimen, she must have left some beauties behind – they should lead us to the eggs."

That was a great idea, so the three of them spread out across the beach looking for signs of turtle flippers in the sand.

"Look there," shouted Sammy, jumping up and down with little crab jumps.

"Two at a time big prints in the sand – it must have been Mrs Turtle from earlier!"

And he was right; they definitely looked like flipper prints from a very large turtle. They followed the prints until they stopped at a mound of sand. Millie swiped away the top layer of sand to reveal a pile of very large eggs.

Harry was elated and sprinted back to where Mrs Turtle was waiting. "Mrs Turtle, Mrs Turtle! We've found your eggs, follow me, come on!"

He jogged back (not sprinting as turtles aren't that quick on land) with Mrs Turtle crawling behind.

When she saw the eggs Mrs Turtle clapped her flippers together and lay on top of the nest, as if giving eggs a lovely big hug.

"Thank you so much," she said to the children and Sammy. "I'm not sure I would ever have found my eggs without your help. Can I do something for you?"

Sammy spoke quickly and first. "Oh, errr, could I have an egg? Or a cuddle? Anything would be good really."

Millie crouched down in front of the crab. "Sammy, that was really nice of you, helping us help Mrs Turtle. Here, have these back," and she held out the glasses they had confiscated earlier.

"Thanks, girl," said Sammy, and put them back on.

"Ooooohhhh, that's not a turtle, it's a crocodile!" he said, and scuttled off back to his rocks.

The children giggled; perhaps those glasses weren't right for Sammy either – he seemed to see worse with them than without!

"Actually Mrs Turtle, we do need some help," said Millie as she sat down next to her on the sand.

"My toy rabbit is stuck on that rock out there –' she pointed – 'and we can't swim that far. Can you please help us?"

"Of course I can," said Mrs Turtle. "Get on my back and you can ride on my shell, rescue your bunny and I'll bring you back to shore. Come on!"

The turtle shell was a bit slippery but the children held on tight and they launched out to sea, bobbing up and down in the surf. Their legs were soaked every time a wave came in, but they were soon there and Millie climbed off the turtle's back onto the rocks and held out her arms, which the rabbit leapt into.

"Poor rabbit – you're so cold and wet. We'll wrap you up in a towel as soon as we get back," comforted Millie, and hugged it tightly.

Harry and the turtle were waiting and Millie and the rescued passenger climbed back on board and they were soon heading back to the beach.

When they landed on shore the children dismounted and walked back to the eggs with the turtle.

"Thank you so much for helping me find my eggs," she said. "I hope you have a lovely time for the rest of your holiday."

Millie explained. "Mrs Turtle, we aren't actually on a real holiday. That was last year. Now we've travelled back here through a magic Zablet – and we need to go home."

At that very moment back at home, Millie and Harry's dad was out in the garden, trimming shrubs and hedges. He decided to pop along to the playhouse to see what the children were up to. He looked inside the playhouse and was surprised not to see them there. Then he noticed the Zablet on the floor and picked it up.

"Tut-tut. The children really shouldn't be so careless with this," he muttered to himself, and took it back indoors.

When he turned the Zablet back on he could see that the children had been looking at holiday photos from their trip to Mesalonia.

He made himself a cup of tea, and as he was sipping at it swiped through some more of the pictures on the Zablet. As he did so, a message popped up on the screen which read:

> **ZABLET MEMORY**
> **NEARLY FULL. PLEASE**

Dad thought this was probably because he had put so many films and pictures (like the holiday ones) on the Zablet, so he decided it would be a good idea to free up some space by deleting all of the holiday photos. After all, they had them on other computers.

He hovered his finger over the Mesalonia folder, and then tapped it and another box popped up which said:

Now what Dad didn't know was that Millie and Harry were of course inside the magic Zablet, in Mesalonia!

If he deleted those pictures, how would they ever get back? Would they be stuck in the Zablet forever?

Just as Dad was about to bring his finger down on OK (to delete the pictures) the house phone began to ring in the front room.

He put down the Zablet and his cup of tea and walked to the phone and answered it.

"Hello, can I help you?"

"Hello indeed to you, Mr Dad, Daddums, Baddy whatever it was, top of the day, morning and afternoon to you as well," said an excitable and strangely familiar female voice. "And thank you for asking, yes, you can help me, so you can, you can help me very muchly."

"May I ask who this is, if you don't mind?" asked Dad.

"Mind? Would I mind? Hahaha of course not, Mr Dad!" said the lady on the phone.

"Why on earth would I mind? Minding is what minders do, or misery-guts types. You just go right ahead and carry on, and I'll carry on not minding, so I will."

Dad got the impression this lady was quite daft and also wasting his time. He had a cup of tea to drink and, more importantly, shrubs to trim.

At that very moment back in Mesalonia (in the Zablet) Mrs Turtle was leading the children to a small shallow-looking rock pool at the far end of the beach, where the sand stopped at the base of a rocky cliff.

"Jump in," she said pointing a flipper at the children and then the pool.

The children stood over the pool and peered in. It was perfectly still and they could see their reflections, but then the water rippled and within the depths of the pool they could see their front room back at home and their dad talking on the phone.

"Jump in," said Mrs Turtle again. "It's a gateway pool, and the only way I know of to jump through cyberspace in a hurry. I've seen other folk use it."

Millie and Harry held hands, counted to three, jumped in and went straight through, disappearing completely from the beach.

With a double *pop* they pop-popped out of the Zablet right next to where Dad had left it in the kitchen, beside his cup of tea. He was still talking on the phone and hadn't even noticed them appear.

They listened at the door of the front room.

"OK, Madam Twinkle, yes, that's lovely. ...Yes, thank you for checking, I appreciate that very much. ...Yes ... yes ..., yes, very kind of you, I'll be sure to do that ... Yes, bye now ... yes, yes ... byeee. GOODBYE!" and he put down the phone and breathed a huge sigh of relief.

"Oh, hello, kids, where have you been?" said Dad when he saw them, but he didn't wait to hear their answer.

"You won't guess who that was on the phone? You remember the rather strange lady we bought the Zablet from? Remember her? Well, that was her calling to check that everything was OK with it and that we were happy with our purchase. Isn't that nice of her?"

Millie picked up the Zablet from where Dad had left it on the table and noticed he had been about to delete the Mesalonia pictures.

Had Madam Twinkle called for a reason?

Millie left the Zablet alone for a few days, uncertain about what could happen next.

At school they had been learning about Florence Nightingale, and Millie was fascinated by the famous nurse and how she had cared for injured soldiers. She and Harry sometimes played a game, and her little brother was more than happy to play the role of a brave soldier while she was the heroine.

As usual, however, Ethel had been envious of her doing so well in class and had been rude to her, so at dinner time that evening she just sat pushing her food around the plate. Millie usually loved her food, so Mum knew something was wrong.

"I think you should have an early night, darling," she said to Millie, putting an arm round her. "Don't you feel well?"

Millie didn't want to tell her about Ethel because she would worry, so she just nodded glumly.

"OK, Mum," she said glumly. "Can I play on the Zablet before I go to sleep?"

Not remembering what Madam Twinkle had said about never using the Zablet after bedtime, Mum agreed that Millie could use it for ten minutes before sleep-time.

When she had brushed her teeth Mum and Dad came and kissed her goodnight and reminded her again, "Only ten minutes on the Zablet, Millie."

Millie heard Harry complaining that *he* wasn't unwell and didn't want to go to bed yet.

She turned on the Zablet and swiped across to a website that Dad had set up for her which was all about famous people.

Millie began to read about how Florence Nightingale had helped so many wounded soldiers during the Crimean War, which had happened more than one hundred years ago. She wished she could be as brave and valiant, and as she thought this, a strange thing happened.

The Zablet whistled and a message appeared on the screen.

NEW EMAIL RECEIVED

Millie tapped the messaging icon, which looked an envelope. A new message opened on the screen. It said:

FROM: SCHOOL

SUBJECT: HOMEWORK

DO YOU WANT TO MEET FLORENCE NIGHTINGALE?

DO YOU WANT TO BE A REAL NURSE IN HER TEAM?

DO YOU WANT TO WIN A THOUSAND POUNDS?

THEN CLICK HERE!

Millie thought about that proposition for a moment. Meeting Florence Nightingale sounded great. She also knew a thousand pounds was a lot of money. Imagine what fun she could have and things she could buy for her family.

But would school send her such a message? She hadn't heard of such a thing before. And would they offer her money too?

It did sound suspicious, but so tempting.

She listened for a minute. Mum and Dad had gone downstairs and Harry now seemed to be asleep in his room.

Millie placed her (writing) hand on the screen, closed her eyes and counted …

As she was tired she began to slowly drift off to sleep, dreaming of Florence's heroics, helping wounded soldiers in Scutari and being very brave.

Suddenly she was awoken by screaming and shouting and terrifying loud *bang*s.

Millie was still lying down in a bed. That much was the same. But it was not her own bed and she was in a large room lit dimly by flickering light.

People were running and shouting in all directions, and as she looked around there were rows of other beds, all with people in, and she realised they were soldiers, lying wounded in the beds, shouting out, begging, for a nurse to help them.

If the noise wasn't enough the horrid smell made Millie rise from her bed, covering her mouth and nose with her hand.

A nurse passed by and said to her kindly, "Oh, you brave soul, you must lie down and get some more rest, a nurse will be with you soon."

Millie lay back down again.

The nurse hurried off and Millie rose from her bed once again. In the bed next to hers lay an injured soldier.

He looked at her with tired, bloodshot eyes and gasped, "Please, some water."

Millie saw a jug on a table on the other side of the room and went to get it. It was full to the brim with water and she returned to the soldier.

"Sit up," she said, propping a couple of cushions so he could do so comfortably.

"Thank you," rasped the soldier as he gulped the water from a cup Millie had poured it into.

"Welcome to Scutari," he said.

More shouting made Millie turn to a bed opposite.

"My leg hurts so much. More bandages, please," said another wounded man.

This place was truly horrific and Millie wasn't sure if she wanted to be here any more.

She went off in search of bandages. The hall was chaotic, nurses running here, there and everywhere, soldiers screaming and shouting in pain.

Finally Millie saw a roll of bandages in a cupboard, and as she went to grab them there was another huge *bang* and they were plunged into darkness.

It was so dark Millie couldn't see her hand in front of her face, but still the yells and screams continued all around. She couldn't hear for the noise, but could feel her heart beating very hard and fast.

She held onto a table to retain some sense of where she was.

And it was then she noticed a dim glow at the other end of the long room, which began to gently flicker and move nearer, towards her. It was such a warm comforting glow – yes, it was a lamp being carried by someone – and it was drawing ever nearer.

Millie was hypnotised by the light; it was such a kind, soothing light. She wasn't scared any more, and as it came nearer she could make out the faint outline of a lady, and the dancing flame in the lamp flickered against the lady's face.

She was smiling softly, and from the panic and terror a calm swept over Millie. The lady was wearing a nurse's uniform.

She stopped in front of Millie and smiled.

"Who are you and why are you in my hospital?" she asked.

"I'm a girl … but … but … I'm not from here," stuttered Millie. "I don't belong here."

"Yes, I can see that," said the nurse. "What is your name, child?"

"Millie," said Millie.

"Well, I'm very pleased to meet you, Millie," said the lady with the lamp.

"My name is Florence. Florence Nightingale."

"How do you do?" asked Florence ever so politely, and extended her hand (the one not holding the lamp)

The shouting and screaming had subsided. Millie closed her eyes in disbelief and then opened them again.

Yes, Florence Nightingale was standing right in front of her!

The lights flickered and came back on and Millie could see the horror around them once again. The wounded soldiers writhing in agony, the nurses and doctors hurriedly scampering about carrying things and tending to this patient and that.

"I'm scared, Nurse Florence," said Millie. "This isn't what I thought would happen."

Florence smiled softly again. "I know, Millie. But you have been so very valiant, tending to the wounded soldiers. Why did you come? Who sent you?"

Millie didn't want to say, at least not about the money.

"I wanted to meet you, Florence, and work in your hospital. I thought it would be an amazing adventure," she said – at least that part was honest.

"It's not fun though, is it?" asked Florence.

"No, I'm very scared," Millie said, trembling. "There are so many people hurt and suffering here."

"Scutari during the Crimean War is a very frightening place, Millie," said Florence.

"Of course, so is any war. Come and take a look." Florence led Millie by the hand to a window.

"Look," she said, and opened the window so they could peer out into the dark night, the flashes blinding them, caused by the constant flares and explosions.

An intense smell of burning matches poured in through the window. That, and the cold air, blasts, blinding flashes and shouting almost overwhelmed Millie.

She saw a group of soldiers in uniforms firing musket guns into the distance at an unseen enemy. There was a lull in the firing, and for a brief moment there was silence before another a loud *boom* rattled her ears and the soldiers suddenly looked terrified; some tried to turn and run, others dived to the floor, but it was too late as a cannonball came hurtling through the night sky towards them.

It was truly too horrible to watch as it plunged into the middle of the group and Millie covered her eyes.

She flinched away from the window, but to her horror she saw another soldier writhing in pain in a bed opposite. But she recognised this soldier. How could this be possible? He was supposed to be asleep in his own bed.

It was Harry.

"Help! Help!" he bawled feverishly.

Millie panicked. Harry looked in terrible pain. Did he need water? Bandages? Medicine?

Millie felt a hand on her shoulder and saw the familiar soothing glow of the lamp.

"I'll see to him," said Florence, and she sat herself on a chair next to Harry's bed.

She wrung a flannel over a bowl and pressed it to his forehead. Immediately Harry seemed to stop struggling and closed his eyes, as if he had gone back to sleep.

"Do you know this soldier?" asked Florence as she turned her head to Millie.

"Yes. He's my brother," replied Millie.

"Then we must get you both back from whence you came," declared Florence. "As soon as your brother's temperature has reduced and he is well enough to stand, we must return you. Before others you love are pulled in."

"What does that mean, Florence?" pleaded Millie.

"Why has Harry been pulled in? He wasn't even using the Zablet with me."

"I believe it's a virus," explained Florence.

"For many years in my medical journals I have researched and discussed the possible existence of such a virus. A virus so virulent and cunning that it could be passed or transmitted between humans simply by their reading the same book or even looking at the same picture."

"Or by looking at the same Zablet?" asked Millie.

"Well, I'm sure I don't know what a Zablet is, Millie," said Florence. "But never mind – I have developed a medicine for precisely this eventuality."

Florence led Millie to a beautiful and ornate medicine chest. There were at least fifty tiny drawers decorated elegantly with pearl fronts.

Florence took a small notebook from her pocket. "Let me see. The fourth drawer from the left on the third row …" and she opened it and removed two small green pills.

"You will take one and we will give the other to your brother," instructed Florence.

They poured some water from a dented, battered tin jug and walked back to Harry's bed. He seemed to be sleeping.

Florence calmly poured a drop of water into his mouth and popped the pill in.

Immediately Harry coughed in shock and sat bolt upright, almost choking as he did. And then, in an instant, he disappeared!

Another nurse came running over to Millie and Florence, crying, "An empty bed, an empty bed! I have a poor wounded soldier who needs it. Out of the way, please!"

They jumped aside as another soldier covered in mud, soot and blood hobbled across and collapsed onto the bed where Harry had lain only seconds before.

"Oh, Florence," said Millie as she clutched the pill Florence had given her in her hand. "It's such a great honour to have met you, but this is just too terrible for me. I want to go home."

"You are a young girl, Millie," said Florence as she put an arm on her shoulder. "And a war hospital is no place for a child. It should be no place for anyone, but it is what it is.

"There is a lesson here for you, young Millie," continued Florence. "It may have sounded fantastic, but going back in time to meet me? And win money?" she said.

Millie gasped. *How did Florence know about the money?*

"Millie listen to me. If something seems too good to be true, then it most probably is. Meeting me wasn't what you thought it would be – there was no money, and a virus very nearly sucked your entire family in."

Millie nodded to indicate she understood what Florence was saying and hugged her. She held out her hand for the tin cup of water and the nurse passed it gently to her.

Millie gulped the water and the pill and she was gone.

Florence rose from her seat and poured some water for the new patient.

"Keep safe, young Millie," she whispered into the night.

If you had a magic Zablet, what would you use it for? This was precisely the dilemma Millie had as she pondered what she would do next.

Millie had certainly learned a lesson with Florence.

People offering you things you didn't ask for, things that seem so amazingly brilliant – it's probably too good to be true in the real world, and in the cyber-world inside the Zablet, it's probably a trick.

Millie crept from her bedroom to check on Harry and found him snoring away in his bed, and when she came down to breakfast the following morning he was telling Dad about the strangest dream he had ever had. He had been a brave wounded soldier, and not only that – he had been tended to by a nurse called Florence. Who would have thought it?!

Now, what Millie *had* realised about the Zablet was that time seemed to freeze in the real world when you were in the cyber-world. No matter how long you had been away, it was still there or thereabouts when you came back. Nobody even noticed you had been gone.

It was enchanted indeed, so Millie decided to sneak the Zablet into her schoolbag that day and show her best friends, Theo and Nancy, just how magic it was.

Perhaps they could sneak off to a very safe and quick adventure and get back in an instant?

The bell rang for morning break and the children in Millie's class ran out of the door in a mad rush to get out into the sun-bathed playground.

Nancy and Theo stayed behind however, because Millie had told them earlier that she had something special to show them. Theo was unsure about this as he really did want to get outside to do some climbing, but Millie was his best friend so he gave her the benefit of the doubt.

"Look," said Millie, as she pulled the shiny black Zablet from her bag and placed it on the table where it seemed to sparkle.

"Wow!" said Nancy.

"Awesome!" said Theo.

Millie showed them how you could swipe through games and apps and look at photos, and then she took pictures of them while they pulled silly faces.

"Now, you mustn't tell anyone about *this* bit," whispered Millie as she looked around to check nobody else could hear.

She tapped on an app called InstaPic (where you can look at photos your friends have taken and they can look at yours) and spoke quietly. "Nancy, you hold my hand, and Harry, you hold Nancy's hand."

"This is getting a bit silly now, Millie," huffed Nancy.

Once InstaPic was loaded there was a picture of Millie's cousin at the circus on the screen. They were "friends" on InstaPic.

This could be fun, thought Millie.

She placed her writing hand on the screen and said to the others, "Just trust me. Close your eyes while I count."

"Super-silly now," chipped in Nancy.

Millie glared at her, so Nancy and Theo did what they were told, to humour her as much as anything, and she began counting …

The roar of a crowd startled them into opening their eyes and they were absolutely astonished to find themselves in the middle of a circus ring!

From behind them a voice bellowed, "Aaaaannnnnd next we have our three helpers, Millie, Nancy and Theeeeoooooohhh!" and the children turned to see a circus ringmaster proudly introducing them to the crowd.

There was so much to take in.

Above them a trapeze artist swung from hoop to hoop up high in the roof of the circus tent.

A man on a unicycle rode around the circus ring again and again, throwing roses into the crowd.

A clown with a big red nose and ridiculous long shoes bounded over to them.

"Hi! I'm Pepe. Hold these," he chortled, and handed them each a water-filled balloon.

CLICK! CLICK! Millie heard the sound of a camera from somewhere. Nobody else seemed to notice.

The clown ran to the other side of the ring as the ringmaster described to the crowd how the three children would throw the balloons to the clown and he would catch them – in his mouth!

It was Nancy's turn first and the ringmaster counted down "Three … two … one!" at which point Nancy hurled her balloon towards the clown with all her might.

Well, the clown tried to catch the rather large balloon with his mouth, but as you might have guessed, it was too big and it simply hit him in the face and burst, soaking him from head to toe.

The crowd roared with laughter.

CLICK! CLICK! There was that camera sound again.

Next it was Theo's turn. Millie noticed a little man at the side, snapping away with a camera, taking pictures of their every action. He was wearing a badge which she squinted to read and could just make out the words 'PAPPA RATZY'. An odd name, thought Millie, but it is a circus.

Theo flung his balloon in the direction of the clown, which of course had the same result, bursting on his head and causing rapturous laughter from the audience as the clown staggered around, spluttering and wiping water from his face.

CLICK! CLICK!

"And noooowwww perhaps our final helper can successfully get the balloon in Pepe's mouth," announced the ringmaster.

The crowd enthusiastically cheered back encouragement.

Millie threw her balloon, two-handed, high up into the air, and as it came down the clown made a big wobbling fuss underneath, and then it vanished!

CLICK! CLICK! There goes that camera.

The clown raised his arms for applause, but the crowd and Millie laughed even more as it was plain for everybody to see that he had simply slipped it down his top. As the unicyclist came round again, he stopped, dismounted and approached the clown.

"What is unicycle-man up to?" the ringmaster asked the crowd.

The unicycle-man walked across to the ringmaster and whispered in his ear.

"Pepe is hiding the balloon, you say?" bellowed the ringmaster as he looked open-mouthed at the crowd in mock-surprise. "Pepe is cheating, you say? He didn't really swallow the balloon?"

Pepe desperately waved his arms and gestured that this just wasn't true.

"Well, if that's the case, we must test him," said the ringmaster, as he removed the flower pinned to his gleaming jacket and walked across to Millie, handing her the flower, the back of which had a pin.

"Young lady," said the ringmaster, "It was your balloon, so please go and prod Pepe in the tummy with this pin."

Pepe looked horrified when he heard "pin" and "prod" and "tummy" in the same sentence as his name.

"Nooo, please no poke me!" he pleaded. "It's-a my tummy, I like-a my tummy not to be poked."

Millie understood this was all a bit of fun and gestured to the crowd as if to ask them, "Shall I poke him with the pin?"

There were a few shouts of "No, leave him alone," as Pepe pretended to shake and shiver in mock-terror, but the majority of the crowd urged Millie on. "It's in his top! Poke him in the tummy!"

Millie theatrically approached Pepe, holding the pin up in the air.

CLICK! CLICK! Pappa Ratzy was busy.

Despite Pepe's protests Millie poked the pin in his tummy and the concealed balloon burst, soaking him even more as the water exploded down him. The crowd roared even harder as the clown's fake tears fell.

More muttering from the crowd and Millie and Nancy looked up. Theo had found a ladder propped against one of the poles holding up the circus tent, and was climbing up to where a trapeze artist was holding out her hand to help him.

"Millie! Nancy! Look at me!" he shouted down as he carefully made his way across the tightrope, which went from one side of the circus ring to the other.

Now, Theo was very good at climbing but he was also very clumsy. Concentrating extremely hard he put forward his right foot, then his left foot, then right, then left.

Millie and Nancy were cheering him on and the crowd held their breath. He had reached almost halfway when he saw down below a fire-eater warming up (despite getting very warm indeed due to eating fire, which is of course very hot, a fire-eater still needs to rehearse their act) and the sight of it distracted him.

Left foot, right foot, left foot … It should have been right foot but Theo wasn't watching the rope any more and … oops!

His right foot found only thin air as he suddenly lurched forward. He tried to grab the rope, but it all happened too quickly and Theo plummeted towards the ground.

Millie was open-mouthed. Nancy screamed like a banshee.

Fortunately Pepe had stopped crying. Showing there were no hard feelings, he pushed his trampoline towards the spot where Theo was going to land. Theo hit the centre of the trampoline very hard and catapulted back up into the air.

The crowd cheered again, thinking it was all part of the act, and the girls breathed a huge sigh of relief.

Theo, still bouncing up and down, began striking different funny poses as the crowd hooted and chanted, "More! More! More!"

This was a lot of fun!

The ringmaster took to the microphone again. "And nooowww for our next act – Mrs Magisto, the amaaaazinnnng knife thrower!"

Mrs Magisto looked very familiar to Millie. She was dressed in a glamorous sparkling silver bodysuit but also sported a multicoloured headscarf with very big earrings and a lot of jewellery.

When Theo finished bouncing on the trampoline he joined the girls again and the ringmaster asked, "Which of these brave children will volunteer to have knives thrown at them by the wonderfully talented Mrs Magisto?"

"Enough already," whispered Nancy to the other two. "I don't know about you but I am *not* having knives thrown at me by anyone, even if she is a fantastic aim and wonderfully talented. Let's go back *right now*, Millie."

"Time for us to go, I'm afraid, Mr Ringmaster," said Millie.

The ringmaster looked horrified. "But, children," he argued, "the show must go on," and as they looked to the exit they could see that the circus strongman was now blocking it off.

They were trapped.

"I'll volunteer," said Millie bravely, and strode forward to the wooden wheel to which she would be attached.

"Millie, no," pleaded Theo and Nancy, but it was too late and the crowd cheered as Millie approached.

Mrs Magisto began to tie Millie to the wheel, which would then slowly rotate while she threw knives at the parts where Millie's arms or legs (hopefully) weren't going to be.

As she was tying Millie to the wheel Mrs Magisto leaned forward and softly whispered – with a voice Millie had heard before, "I've only tied the ropes very loosely, Millie. Upon my signal, all three of you are to run out of the exit. And don't look back."

Mrs Magisto went back to her starting position across the circus ring and a hush settled over the crowd as the ringmaster described how terribly dangerous this act was going to be.

Nancy and Theo were rigid with horror.

The wheel began to slowly turn and Mrs Magisto pulled back her arm and threw the first knife.

However, rather than hitting the wheel or going anywhere near Millie, it sailed straight over her and stuck into a rope which was supporting one of the tightrope poles.

The knife sheared through the rope and it pinged apart. Every single person under the circus tent watched in horror as the pole began to teeter and tip towards one section of the crowd. People screamed and ran for cover as the pole began its descent.

"Strongman Igor here!" came a deep booming shout as the circus strongman leapt into action, dashing across the circus ring to catch the huge pole as it came crashing down.

"Strongman Igor save day!" he proudly declared as he held the pole aloft like a trophy.

"Quick! Now! Children, run!" shouted Mrs Magisto at Millie, Theo and Nancy as she pointed at exit, which was now clear.

The children didn't need to be told twice and they fled the circus ring and ran down the passage marked 'EXIT'.

And they didn't look back either.

They stood in the dark outside the circus tent, listening to the commotion going on inside.

"So how do we get back home exactly?" asked Nancy.

"I'm not sure," replied Millie. "There always seems to be a way though – you just have to look for it."

Theo chipped in. "Let's search around the outside of the tent. Maybe we'll find something."

The children began to work their way around, carefully feeling their way in the dark, past the tent ropes and wooden stakes securing the ropes in the grass.

"Halt!" shouted a gruff voice, making the children jump with fright. "Who goes there?"

They turned and a torch shone a bright light their way, blinding them momentarily.

Once they became used to the light they could make out that it was a policeman addressing them. "What are you up to, snooping around the circus?"

Millie tried to speak, but the policeman continued, "Had a lot of trouble around here lately, we have. I expect you were looking to break into the circus? See the show for nothing? I'm placing you all under arrest," and he blew hard on his whistle.

Before the children could do or say a thing, more policemen appeared from all directions and surrounded them. The first policeman pointed to a big white police van and marched them into it.

They drove through the dark night. In the back of the van, Nancy was getting hysterical.

"Millie! We've been arrested! I'm going to be in *soooo* much trouble! I'm a good girl really, I've been trying *soooo* hard! This is terrible! Awful! Get us out of this. Now!"

"Quiet in the back there," shouted one of the policemen in the front, and the children hushed as they watched to see where they were being taken.

They arrived outside a large and impressive old building with the word 'COURTHOUSE' written in large letters above the huge wooden doors.

The children were marched into the building and told to join a queue of people, all looking either thoroughly miserable or distressed.

At the front of the queue were three very fat people, two men and a lady.

"NEXT TO GO BEFORE THE BARMY JUDGE!" shouted a dwarf with a loudspeaker, standing by a doorway to another room.

To their right was a window looking into that room, and at the front facing the rest of the room was a red-faced angry-looking man with a curly white wig and a hammer. This must be the barmy judge. The children watched as the three fat people trooped slowly in and sat down on a bench facing him.

"You are brought before this court today, charged with eating too much exquisite food," stated the judge.

The fatter of the two men spluttered, "But … what … but … how did you know?"

"The pictures were on InstaPic, you fool!" screamed the judge. "There for all to see. On InstaPic there are pictures of EVERYTHING you do!"

"Just last night pictures of your fish-and-chip supper, delicious looking, with peas and tartare sauce," vented the enraged judge. "With a cheeky slice of lemon."

The fat group were astonished as he continued. "The previous day, this gluttonous group feasted upon a cake each at lunchtime. A cake no less!"

The group looked at each other open-mouthed.

"I suggest shutting those excessive big mouths before someone puts food in there, getting you into even more trouble!" barked the judge.

"But there's no law against having nice food," protested the fattest of the three.

"Silence!" barked the judge. "I am the barmy judge and I will interpret the law as I so please. And I so please to sentence you to a month in prison, with only lettuce to eat."

An evil smirk creased across his face. "Bhahahaaaa, only lettuce, just like little rabbits. Perhaps other prisoners can throw some carrots for you on Fridays! Bahaaaahaaaaahaaaaa … AWAY WITH THEM NOW!" he shouted, as policemen led the podgy threesome off weeping, to some unseen prison.

"NEXT TO BE HEARD BY THE BARMY JUDGE!" shouted the dwarf with the loudspeaker, and as the queue shuffled up one place Millie and her friends gasped as a small fairy fluttered into the courtroom and hovered in front of the bench.

"Ah yes … erm … the fairy … now … erm … let me see … what heinous crime is it you have committed?" mumbled the judge as he looked the fairy up and down.

"Turning a goblin to ice perhaps?" asked the fairy, who looked very angry.

"Ah yes, thank you, my dear," said the judge.

"Yes indeed, the ice goblin. Terrible business that. Dreadful. And then you thought to put a picture on InstaPic? As if to gloat about your terrible crime?"

The fairy's eyes widened. "That was how I was caught? InstaPic?! Well, nobody in the village seemed to mind. That horrid goblin was tricking children into giving him their passwords – for empty packets of sweets. He deserved it! And he will be fine once he thaws. Hopefully he will have learnt a lesson."

"Hmmm, yes," mused the judge. "He is a contemptuous and spiteful little goblin, that one, it must be said. I've had him here in my court several times."

He pulled a large red book from under his seat, blew the dust from it and began flicking through the pages far too quickly to be actually reading them.

76

His head suddenly popped back up from searching through the book. "Little fairy, had you not chosen to share your handiwork with the entire InstaPic multiverse, nobody need have known about your actions," he spoke quite calmly now.

"But you did and I have found a law in the ancient barmy book of barmy rules against turning vicious goblins into ice – they make a terrible mess when they melt."

The judge's voice began to rise again. "And I don't like terrible messes! Or frozen goblins! And a review of the pictorial evidence makes it clear you are guilty of both. Therefore as the perpetrator of the crime I hereby SENTENCE YOU TO ONE MONTH WITH YOUR WINGS TIED TOGETHER!"

The fairy looked aghast and quickly tried to dart towards the door and out, but the judge leapt up from his seat, produced a huge long stick with a net attached and like a fisherman thrust out the net, trapping the fairy before she could get away.

"Noooo! Pleeasse! Not my wings!" she pleaded tearfully, but it was too late, and another policeman tied a knot in the net and whisked her away.

The children watched as more cases were heard, all convicted of their supposed crimes based on evidence from pictures posted on InstaPic. Finally the three of them were at the front of the queue as a distraught sailor was marched off for sailing his boat on water, sentenced by the barmy judge to a week of seasickness.

"NEXT BEFORE THE BARMY JUDGE …" bellowed the dwarf, "the clown fraternisers!"

The children slouched into the courtroom..

"The very worst of crimes," exclaimed the excited judge. "Playing with clowns," and he pointed to a screen on the wall as pictures of Millie, Theo and Nancy were shown playing with Pepe the clown at the circus.

"An open-and-shut case if I ever saw one," declared the judge. "What have you to say for yourselves?"

"We didn't know it was wrong to play with clowns," pleaded Millie.

"Ignorance is no excuse," barked the judge. "When you are in InstaPic, EVERYTHING is seen and there are many different opinions. There is no telling who will like – or otherwise – what it is you have done."

"We aren't even from this place," shouted Theo, getting more and more upset at their seemingly predetermined fate.

"You are in InstaPic, so your pictures, they … are ALWAYS HERE," laughed the judge.

"I hereby find you guilty of fraternising and socialising with clowns. Playing with horrific unscrupulous painted-face beasts! I'm not sure there is even a law against it, but I hate clowns! I sentence you to one month in prison, in the world of InstaPic! No going home for you, children! Baahaahaahahaaaa! Smile for camera on the way out, won't you? Say, 'Cheese!'"

The children were led out of the door and out of the courthouse by a group of policemen – an explosion of flashes went off as a gaggle of people, all equipped with Pappa Ratzy badges and cameras, clicked away.

"Oh my goodness," wept Nancy. "We're being pictured and tagged going to prison. My mum and dad will see it and my new well-behaved reputation will be worthless. I'm ruined."

Back in the police van Millie turned to the others. "We need to find a way out of this."

"Can't we just climb out of a window and escape?" whispered Nancy hopefully.

"No, you saw what they did to the fairy who tried to get away," said Millie.

"I don't want my wings clipped, thank you very much." Nancy looked hopeful suddenly. "But we don't have wings!"

Millie's gaze set her back again. "Then they would tie something else together like our legs. Something that would bother us just as much as having wings tied together upset the fairy."

Theo, who had been reading something on the back of a seat, put his hands on their shoulders and whispered, "It says here on this poster that as InstaPic has fair laws, we can request a retrial at any time."

"What's the point of that?" asked Millie. "You saw that barmy judge. I don't want to go in front of him again – he would just sentence us to prison again … and next time he might throw away the key."

"Not if we can delete the pictures," said Theo with a mischievous glint in his eye.

Theo explained his plan to the others. It was good but with one major flaw. To send an email to someone in the real world they needed a device capable of doing so. A Zablet, a phone, another type of computer, anything.

But the children had nothing like this.

When the van arrived at the gloomy-looking prison they were taken in through the front door where a stern man in a police uniform with a large moustache glared at them: "I'm the desk sergeant. I'll need your details."

He pushed out three pieces of paper with dotted lines on which to write their names, addresses and dates of birth. At the bottom of the sheet was an empty box labelled "Fingerprint".

When they had finished the written details the gruff desk sergeant put a blue ink pad in front of them.

"Press your forefinger in the pad, get it nice and inky and then press it in the box there, please."

That was the first time he had said *please*, but at least he had said it, so Millie thought, , perhaps he wasn't so bad after all.

"Could I have some water, please, Mr Policeman?" asked Theo suddenly, sounding very raspy. "I'm really thirsty after the stress of the court and the police van."

The desk sergeant fixed a grumpy stare at Theo before his features suddenly softened and he replied, "Yes, of course, laddie, I'll get you a drink." He turned round to a water fountain behind his desk.

Theo grabbed Millie and Nancy by the shoulder again, his eyes wide open, and he whispered very quietly so the desk sergeant couldn't hear, "Listen, I'm switching our paper sheets around. These forms have our *personal information* on, and with a fingerprint too. Someone could use that to impersonate us here or in cyberspace. I've heard my dad talk about it. We really don't want them matching our fingerprints to our names and birthdays, especially after what they've done with pictures of us."

He checked the desk sergeant wasn't coming back. "Let's swap them now."

The girls nodded that they understood, and while the desk sergeant's back was still turned they quickly exchanged them and then each went about putting their fingerprint on the sheet that was now in front of them.

Millie put her print on Theo's sheet, Nancy put hers on Millie's and Theo applied his inky finger to Nancy's prison sheet.

The desk sergeant turned around before they had a chance to switch the sheets back again and placed a glass of water in front of Theo.

"There you go, errrrrr …" he said, glancing down at the sheet in front of Theo and then looking back at him rather surprised. "Errrrr … Nancy? Is that your name, boy? Isn't that a girl's name?"

As Theo gulped down the water, trying to buy time to think, Nancy chipped in suddenly. "It's a place in France. His parents went there before he was born and really liked it, so he got the name. It never bothered them for a minute to think that it was also a girl's name, and a lovely girl's name it is too. Don't you think, Mr Desk Sergeant?"

"Yes, um, I suppose it is a pretty name, errr … Millie," said the desk sergeant as he checked the name on the sheet in front of Nancy.

As he collected up the sheets he glanced at them and then looked up again, startled, at Millie.

"Theo?" he asked, exasperated at another irregular name. "Isn't that a boy's—"

"Short for Theresa," interrupted Nancy before anyone else had a chance to open their mouth.

"OK," said a now very bemused-looking desk sergeant. "I suppose that is, errr … all correct then. I'll show you to your cell, in that case, if there are no other requests?"

They began to walk down the huge, wide, bright white corridor. Either side every few steps was a large iron door to a cell. They heard sobbing coming from behind one of them.

"Only lettuce … *sob*! I want a cake … *sob*! Please, can anyone hear me?"

The desk sergeant peered through the bars in the door and shouted, "Quiet in there! If you hadn't been so silly as to put pictures up of everything you did and where you did it, you wouldn't be in this bother!"

While the desk sergeant was ranting through the bars Theo carefully tiptoed up behind him and gently lifted his police radio from his belt. This was a very fancy radio with a screen and Theo was sure it looked like one that could send email. He tucked it behind his back.

Another few doors down was an open door and the desk sergeant showed the children into their cell. There was a bunk bed and a single bed, a TV, a sofa and a fridge. It was quite comfortable-looking, but they were still being locked up and unable to go home. This wasn't good.

"Sorry about this, kids," sympathised the desk sergeant. "But you really must think more about all these photos going onto InstaPic or wherever else they go; you never know who is looking at them or what they might do with them."

Clank! The door slammed shut.

"You get meals at eight o'clock in the morning, midday, four in the afternoon and seven in the evening before lights out," he shouted back through the bars, and they heard his footsteps going off down the corridor.

Nancy threw herself down on one of the beds. "It's awful," she wailed. "We're never going to get out of here. I want to go home!"

"Let's not give up just yet, Nancy," said a grinning Theo as he produced the police radio from behind his back. "I'm going to send an email."

"Who to?" asked Millie. "Who can help us get out of this mess?"

"Geeky Gavin," replied Theo, frantically tapping away on the screen.

The girls' eyes lit up because they knew that this was a very good idea indeed.

Geeky Gavin was *always* using his Zablet. He would no doubt be sitting in a corner of the playground right now doing something very geeky while the other children ran around him, jumping, screaming, laughing and generally having fun, as if he wasn't there.

They looked at what Theo had written on the screen:

Hi Gav!

It's Theo here. No time for questions – I need you to do me a really big favour.

On the floor in the classroom you will see Millie Tyler's Zablet.

Please pick it up and go to her InstaPic app.

Delete any pictures you can see of us with clowns.

Thanks a lot,

Theo.

He hit Send.

At that moment Gavin was indeed sitting in a corner of the playground, away from all the noise and commotion of the other children playing, his own Zablet on his lap, trying to work out how to code an app.

Gavin was very clever.

A familiar *whoosh* broke his concentration and a box popped up on the screen.

> **NEW MESSAGE**
> **RECEIVED**

Hmmm. Interesting, thought Gavin. He didn't usually get emails during the school day, except from his father, who was also always on his computer and sometimes needed advice.

Gavin opened the mail app and Theo's message appeared. Gavin read the message and absorbed it. Gavin wasn't prone to excitement, but he was quite intrigued by the prospect of having a snoop around Millie's Zablet.

He rose from where he was sitting, carefully placed his Zablet into its case and crept towards the classroom.

Just as Theo had said in his email, the Zablet was there on the floor. Gavin picked it up and turned it on. It was as the children had left it, with InstaPic open on the screen.

Gavin carefully scrolled down the pictures on display, occasionally raising an eyebrow as he saw Nancy hurling a water balloon at a clown, Millie about to have knives thrown at her and Theo on a tightrope.

He was about to have a further poke around when he heard the *whoosh* sound again.

Gavin was again curious enough to be distracted from his primary task and opened up his mail app again.

Hi again, Gav!

It's Theo again. Please delete ALL pictures. Especially any pictures with fairies freezing goblins.

Not just ones with clowns.

Thanks.

Considering the different options available to him, Gavin thought about *not* deleting the pictures and instead using Millie's Zablet to see if it was like his one.

Was it as powerful? As clever? Had it been as well optimised?

Probably not, he decided. He also added to the equation the fact that Theo was generally quite nice to him, often inviting him to "Get off his backside and come and play football" even though Gavin never did.

Gavin pressed on the picture of Nancy throwing the balloon at a clown and pressed the dustbin button.

ARE YOU SURE YOU
WANT TO DELETE THE
PICTURE?

Gavin chose YES. He then did the same for all of the other pictures with Millie, Theo and Nancy in a circus which was more or less what Theo had asked. An odd request, thought Gavin, but he did know a lot about the cyber-world and concluded Theo was likely being cautious and didn't want pictures up on InstaPic of him and his friends at a circus when they should be at school.

Hang on a minute. They had been at school right before playtime, hadn't they?

"Give it ten minutes," said Theo to the girls. "Then we'll call the desk sergeant back."

It took an age to pass, but eventually the children started banging their fists on the door and calling out, "Mr Desk Sergeant, you dropped your radio!"

It didn't take long before they heard footsteps running down the corridor and the jangle of keys in the lock. The door swung open.

"Thanks, kids," said the thrilled desk sergeant, not at all grumpy now. "I've been looking for this everywhere."

"It must have fallen out of your pocket while you locked us up," said Millie, winking at the others.

"Yes, I suppose it must have," he said, taking it back. "Are you settling in OK? Is there anything I can do?" he asked.

Nancy spoke up. "Well, actually there is," she said. "We would like to request a retrial."

"You want to go before the barmy judge again?" asked the very surprised-looking desk sergeant.

"Yes," said Nancy firmly. "We believe the evidence used is not reliable."

The desk sergeant looked at the others and they nodded back in agreement with Nancy.

"Well, I suppose it's your right," he said. "Nobody ever asks for a retrial unless they want their punishment increased, but if you're sure." He opened the door, gesturing for them to follow him out.

They went through everything in reverse. The desk sergeant gave them back their (mixed-up) sheets of paper, they walked out of the prison to be met by the police van, complete with guards. They drove back to the courthouse (not backwards) and were met with another long line of supposed wrongdoers.

In the queue were all manner of creatures and beings. A group of what appeared to be robots stood around whirring and beeping as they waited in the line. Next to them a rock band, complete with guitars and drumsticks. At the front of the queue two bakers were summoned into the courtroom by the dwarf with his loudspeaker.

"NEXT BEFORE THE BARMY JUDGE!" he bellowed and the bakers solemnly trudged forward.

Just as before, the children watched the cases unfold as the barmy judge read out all manner of ludicrous charges against the defendants in the land of InstaPic.

The bakers were charged with baking baguettes and not normal loaves, something the judge found to be extremely troubling.

"A long, thin, stale baguette could be a dangerous weapon," he decreed, and sentenced them.

The rock band were charged with taking selfies up on stage and therefore not fully concentrating on their concert.

The robots were charged with playing games while their human masters were not around.

All had taken pictures of their deeds, uploaded them in InstaPic and were found guilty and sentenced to three weeks in "digital-clink".

"NEXT BEFORE THE BARMY JUDGE!" hollered the dwarf once more, and then quickly added, "LAST CASE

BEFORE LUNCHTIME!" This upset a group of elves who were right behind the children in the queue.

The children hurried into the courtroom.

The barmy judge was intently staring at a computer screen on his desk, probably looking on InstaPic for more offenders, thought Millie. He looked up as the children sat down on the same bench they had sat on just a few hours before.

"You again?" asked the old man, looking surprised.

Millie stood up and addressed him. "Yes, your honour. We have come back before the court to request a retrial."

The judge snorted indignantly. "On what grounds? The evidence was there for all to see. Pictures of your fraternising with painted-face beasts. Clowning with clowns. I decided it's illegal, and the proof of your actions was on InstaPic. With the geolocation added, the police knew precisely where to find you. It's indisputable. Absolute. Incontestable. So I ask you again – ON WHAT GROUNDS?"

"Please look at the pictures again," said Millie calmly.

The barmy judge raised his eyebrows. "Well, this is most unusual, but Rule 4.1, Sub-section 23, Paragraph 1.36 of the InstaPic terms and conditions does indeed state that you are able to contact the authorities and be listened to again. I suppose that includes requests for retrials. Please be seated while I waste my time reviewing the evidence. I could be eating cheese-and-tuna sandwiches, you know."

The children watched as the barmy judge's brow furrowed. Then he frowned, sighed and made a whole series of other gestures indicating something was troubling him as he looked up and down his screen.

After a few minutes or so he looked back up again.

"Extraordinary," he said. "The pictures do appear to be gone. Vanished. Missing. Extinct. Wiped out. Well, I never."

Peering over his glasses, he continued, "In the absence of any evidence to support the accusations, I hereby pardon you of any crimes of which you may have been convicted. You are exonerated and free to go."

The children tried not to let out squeals of delight, but their eyes told how ecstatic they were as they looked at each other; inside they were doing cartwheels of joy.

As the children walked from the courtroom, Theo stopped suddenly and turned back to the barmy judge. "Mr Judge, there was also the case of the fairy – who froze a goblin. Do you remember?"

The judge nodded to indicate that he did, and Theo went on. "Well, can you review that case too, please? I have a feeling another mistake may have been made, and based on the terms and conditions the fairy should be able to have a retrial too."

The judge looked furious and immediately turned back to his screen and began to scroll through the pictures in InstaPic.

Happy that they had set the wheels in motion for the fairy to be released as well, the children left the courthouse.

"How do we get back home now?" asked Nancy.

"Back to the circus," said Millie, and off they stomped.

Once outside Nancy let out an excited squeal. "Look," she said pointing at a sign on a lamppost.

It read CIRCUS THIS WAY with a clown's hand indicating which way to go.

Even as they walked along the streets and roads back to the circus, the *CLICK! CLICK!* of cameras could be heard everywhere. People took pictures of everything in InstaPic!

The circus was very quiet as they approached. There was no show on at the moment.

They slipped into the circus tent under the canopy and entered an empty circus ring. All of the apparatus was arranged, ready for the next performance.

The children looked around, desperately searching for some clue to get back home. This was where they had arrived after all.

"Looking for something?" said a voice concealed in the darkness of the entrance to the circus arena. Millie recognised the voice, but wasn't sure from where.

"I can hear you thinking," said the familiar female voice.

Then out of the darkness strode someone they had indeed seen before. Dressed in sparkling silver with a blindingly colourful headscarf and earrings you could swing from … Yes, it was Mrs Magisto!

Before they could answer she pointed to the centre of the circus ring where a single hoop lay on the ground.

"Stand in that then, children, do hurry," said Mrs Magisto suddenly. Without question they did what she asked.

Once they were in, much to the children's alarm Mrs Magisto produced a flaming torch and touched it to the hoop, which quickly caught fire, creating a circle of flames around them!

The children looked understandably terrified, and Millie shouted, "Mrs Magisto, stop! What are you doing?!"

They were about to leap from the hoop when Mrs Magisto spoke again: "Millie, Theo and Nancy – I hope you've learned some valuable lessons in InstaPic. You're going home now."

They joined hands again, closed their eyes and *POP!*

They were back in the classroom with a gobsmacked Geeky Gavin staring at them.

His prized Zablet bounced on the floor as he fainted in shock.

A few days later, during afternoon playtime at school, Millie, Theo and Nancy were playing a circus game (which given their recent experiences they knew a fair bit about).

Other children joined in the game, but some others who were friendlier with Ethel Morgan were reluctant.

"Millie Tyler," cackled Ethel, "you look like a clown with your feet and ridiculous clothes!"

Ethel's group of followers predictably laughed along, most of them because they were too influenced by her to think for themselves about whether that was actually funny or not.

Despite having what must be the best secret in the world, the constant sniping did upset Millie, who was a nicer person than Ethel.

During her time with the Zablet Millie had begun to occasionally use an app called "CHATTA". You could talk to other children, anywhere in the world, and they were usually much nicer than the likes of Ethel.

Millie had 147 "friends" in CHATTA, none of whom she knew in the real world, but it was fun getting to know people who could be anywhere.

Before you could enter CHATTA you had to pick an avatar – which is the picture of you that others talking to you in CHATTA could see.

Millie knew it wasn't sensible to have real pictures of yourself online if you were a child. Therefore Millie's avatar was of a girl with long golden flowing hair and a bright sky-blue dress and her name was *Ice Princess.*

That evening Millie went up to her bedroom with the Zablet and fired up CHATTA.

Immediately she heard a beep and noticed a box flashing at the bottom of the screen, which meant she had a new message from a CHATTA friend.

She read the message.

Hooky: How ya doing?

Millie replied.

Ice Princess: Not great – a horrible girl at school being nasty to me.

Hooky: That's awful.

Hooky: I'd be horrible back to her for you if I was there. Is she on CHATTA?

(Millie laughed.)

Ice Princess: I don't know, I hope not. I'd hate to bump into her here as well.

Hooky: What's her name? I mean, her real name?

Millie knew she shouldn't say, but she was so angry at Ethel.

Ice Princess: Ethel Morgan.

Hooky was quiet for a time.

Ice Princess: Are you still there, Hooky?

Hooky: Yep.

Hooky: Is that the Morgan family in Springfield Road?

Millie thought that was a strange question, but answered it truthfully; they did live in Springfield Road.

Hooky: I can work out her birthday as 31st October from her parents' FaceSpace pad too. Cool.

95

Millie wasn't quite sure what that meant and where this was now leading to.

Hooky: And also I know you are Millie Tyler of Lloyd Court and your birthday is on the 24th February.

Ice Princess: But … But … How do you know that?

Hooky: Ethel told me.

And with that a hand reached out of the Zablet and pulled Millie right in.

Bright blue sky, a wind whipping against her face and an unsteady floor were the first sensations that hit Millie as she gathered her senses and realised that she needed something to grab on to, quickly.

There was open sea around her in every direction she looked. She was on a boat!

"Ahoy there!" came a voice from above her, and Millie, only able to stay upright because she was clinging onto a railing, looked up.

She could see a man dressed in a white shirt, ragged black trousers cut away above the ankles and a huge black hat. He slid down a pole, which was the mast of the ship, and landed in front of her.

Now Millie could see that on the man's hat was a skull and crossed swords.

This was a pirate ship.

"Captain Jim Hooky," he announced himself proudly and offered his hand. "Pleased to meet you!"

"You … You're Hooky?" asked a puzzled Millie.

"Yep," replied Hooky.

"But … But I thought you were a child, my sort of age," said Millie.

"Yeah, sorry about that," said Hooky. "To be fair, I could have thought you were an ice princess, you know," and he scampered off to the front of the ship.

"Oh, great, now I'm stuck on a pirate ship with the clown girl," said a voice Millie knew all too well, and she looked across the deck to see none other than Ethel Morgan, looking sickly green and clinging to a rail, but still managing to aim a vicious scowl in Millie's direction.

Millie ran after Hooky, holding on to anything she could as she went along to keep her balance on the lurching ship. "What is *she* doing here?" she hissed.

"Well, it's funny you should ask that," said Hooky as he lowered a rope over the front of the ship and then jogged off down the other side of the vessel, seemingly very busy and barely interested in talking to Millie.

But then he stopped, turned around and with a grin told Millie, "It was simple to convince you each to give over the other's personal details, seeing as how the pair of you really don't like each other."

"Once I had those, I could track you down easily, and once your *not-friend* opened up CHATTA on her parents' Zablet … *boom*!" He opened his arms wide and made a grabbing gesture. "We could reach out and pull her in. We did the same to you."

Hooky then produced a telescope, which he opened to its full length and used to study something far out at sea.

"Excellent progress," he chirped. "We'll be there shortly."

His pirate crew busied themselves on the deck, running this way and that.

"Where are we going?" asked Millie. "Where are you taking us?"

"To the all-seeing octopus," replied Hooky, very serious all of a sudden. "The all-seeing octopus has tentacles in every corner of cyberspace. So many corners, so many tentacles!"

"But why?" said Millie.

"You really are full of good questions today, Ice Princess," replied Hooky, fiddling with the telescope. "So much more fun in the flesh than on that CHATTA thing. The all-seeing octopus is where we take all of the personal details we steal."

Millie stared out to the small island in the distance which was looming ever larger. She was about to demand Hooky tell her more about this, but when she looked back he had vanished, or at least she thought he had until she heard him up above, in the crow's nest, surveying all around with his telescope.

"Land ahoy!" he bellowed, as only a pirate would, and the ship came to a slow halt.

Several small rowing boats sailed towards them from the island, pirates paddling them across the crystal-clear water.

"Open up below," ordered Hooky, and Millie watched in amazement as two more pirates opened up hatches in the deck of the ship and from beneath, climbing up steps and shielding their eyes from the sunlight, were more people, obviously also prisoners of the pirates.

There were both grown-ups and children, about twenty in total, some looking quite bemused and some looking very angry indeed.

They were ordered into the rowing boats, each of which had three slats, with room for two to sit on each slat.

Millie was told to get on the last boat. There was just one space left, next to Ethel.

"You stupid idiot, Millie!" snarled Ethel as Millie sat down. "See what you've done?"

"What have I done?" snapped Millie. "*You* did the same, giving my details to Hooky too. And I bet *you* meant to do it; I was tricked."

Ethel looked down suddenly as the boat made its way to the island, and Millie thought she looked perhaps just a little bit ashamed.

"They offered me a treasure chest for your details; I … I tried to sell your information, Millie."

One of the two grown-ups on the slat in front turned round to face them. "They did that to us too! I was promised a crock of gold for giving over my name and other details. Now look where I am!"

"And me!" said another lady. "They promised me designer clothes, they promised me jewellery, but as soon as I gave over my details, *wham bam*, they hooked me in through the screen. It's an outrage!"

On the other boats the passengers all seemed to be angrily discussing the events that had brought them here; some of the children were very upset.

They all had one thing in common though, which was that they or someone else had given their details to the pirates in return for a promise of something.

A large man shouted, "They said they would make my tummy smaller!"

A lady in another boat spoke tearfully. "They said they could turn my dull grey hair lovely and auburn once again."

When the boats were ashore the captives dismounted and were told where to go by various pirates.

Finally the biggest pirate of them all, who also had the biggest sword and the most tattoos, pointed his sword in the direction of a group of trees.

One of the grown-ups refused to go and insisted on being taken back home.

"NOW!" ordered the big pirate, waving his huge sword in the air. Everyone trudged off to where they were told, now too scared to disobey.

Once they had passed through a row of trees the prisoners and their pirate captors came upon a river, which led in one direction into the sea. But upstream a beautiful waterfall, unlike anything Millie had ever seen, cascaded down over the entrance to a cave.

The water seemed to have golden flecks within, flickering like thousands of tiny flames and then sparks where it crashed into the river. It really was like a wall of fire.

"Down the Pyro Waterfall!" shouted Hooky, and as if someone had simply turned off a tap, the pouring fire stopped, leaving the mouth of the cave open.

A mechanical bridge then extended out from the cave to the shore of the river and they were led across it.

Nobody was quite prepared for what was in the depths of the cave. Even Millie was shocked, despite what Hooky had told her.

There in the darkness, staring back at them, was a huge pink octopus.

It was the size of a two-storey house with eyes as big as cars. What was even more remarkable were the tentacles. There weren't just eight of them like an octopus should have. There were literally hundreds. Teeming and wriggling and pointing and flicking, every tentacle seemed to be doing its own thing.

If you followed one tentacle with your eyes you could see it went into the ground; they all went into different holes.

The cleverest-looking pirate unrolled a scroll and began to read from it aloud:

"Jeremy Harper! 15 Darby Road. Date of birth 10th February 1982. Mother's maiden name, Lillywhite!"

They watched as the octopus's eyes widened, then fixed on one particular tentacle. The tentacle quivered for a few seconds, then rose slowly into the air where it hovered and shook for a few seconds more. Then it shot straight out with great force before plunging into the ground.

Millie and Ethel watched as Mr Jeremy Harper of Number 15 Darby Road demanded to know exactly was going on.

"What does that mean? The … the … the … tentacle thing! What that … that … that … thing just did? With my name and address!" he shouted. "It's a scandal!"

Then Mr Harper suddenly looked less angry and more bemused and asked the pirates, "What did it just do then exactly?"

Hooky, who was by far the most talkative of the pirates, strode forward and put his hand on Jeremy Harper's shoulder.

"The mighty, all-seeing, big pink octopus is using your name, address, birth date, mother's maiden name and any other bits we might have turned up," he explained.

"What for?" demanded Jeremy Harper, his rage renewed.

"To impersonate you, silly," chuckled Hooky, who then turned back to the clever pirate. "Next one, Brains."

Jeremy Harper wasn't quite finished. "Why would anyone want to pretend to be me?"

"Oh, don't put yourself down like that," said the pirate captain cheekily. "There are lots of reasons, believe it or not."

Another pirate came forward to explain.

"By pretending to be you in cyberspace, we can sign up for an account as Mr Jeremy Harper on AuctionBay, for instance. Then we can order a new mast for the ship. Ours is falling apart. Very dangerous it is. And the beauty of that is, we don't have to pay for it. YOU DO!"

"You can't do that," stammered Jeremy Harper. "That's fraud!"

"I'm not fond of the word," said Hooky. "But yes, I suppose it is. But hey, we're pirates, it's what we do, and to be honest it beats firing cannons at other ships and sword fighting. That kind of thing is *soooo* last century."

"In fact right now," said the other pirate, "our octopus is impersonating you in FaceSpace, tricking more of your friends – who think we are you – into giving us their details too! It's such a clever idea, you have to admit!"

Hooky repeated. "Brains! Next, please!"

"Martha Higgins. 102a Donnelly Road. Date of birth, 25th December 1979," read out Brains.

Hooky clapped. "Awww … lovely – a Christmas baby."

A tall lady with long blonde hair walked forward looking petrified.

"Mother's maiden name, Lewis. Card number, 3098 0099 8877 6534. Password, fishy1990," continued Brains.

Hooky jumped up and down clapping his hands in glee. "I love these ones! A card number! And a password! Easy peasy ketchup squeezy."

"Why is that so good?" Millie asked Hooky.

"Why? Why, my dear child?" asked Hooky. "Because with Martha over there's card number, we can just take her money without even having to go to all the trouble of pretending to be her. Let me tell you, giving up the seven seas for cyberspace was frankly the best career move I have ever made. This makes taking candy from children look quite challenging!"

Hooky excitedly continued: "And a password! I bet you a jig with the ship's cook that Martha uses that same password everywhere. Soon we'll have access to all of her accounts and apps to do as we Jolly Roger well please!"

Poor Martha fainted when she heard this. Some of the group of prisoners gathered round her. The octopus once again plunged another tentacle into the ground, no doubt cleaning out her bank account.

Millie felt someone standing on the other side of her. Ethel.

"Millie. We have to stop this. I know I can be awful at times, but this is just wrong, and heaven knows what they are going to do with our details when they get to us. They can pretend to be us and pull our friends and family into this too. We need to work together."

Millie knew Ethel was right. But what could they do?

The task was difficult. There were at least ten pirates, most with sharp-looking swords.

Worse still, they were on a desert island with no idea how to get off.

Then Millie had an idea. "We need to build a sign. A big one."

"A sign?" said Ethel. "What of? What for? Is this another one of your stupid—"

"Stop being rude. Working together, remember?" reminded Millie. "I saw a TV show once where the characters who were stuck on a desert island built a huge sign on the beach using branches, sticks and rocks which read: *HELP*. A plane flying above the island saw them and rescued them."

Millie and Ethel slunk away to the back of the group while the pirates read out the details of the next victim.

When the seafaring villains were at their most excited – just when the extent of their plunder was being announced which this time included a PIN number – the two girls slipped away. Fortunately the Pyro-Waterfall hadn't been turned back on so they were able to leave the cave easily enough. They hid behind a rock near the waterfall entrance, watching the goings-on and making sure their absence hadn't been noticed.

Not even Hooky had realised, as he had joined in with a group of his friends singing, drinking, dancing and celebrating the spoils of their lucrative work.

Hey diddly dee!
A pirate's Life for me!
No more taking ships!
Not a bit of it!
We're stealing things for free!

Millie and Ethel knew that was their moment and turned and ran. Down the bridge back to the shore and then through the trees and bushes, they didn't look back, not once.

They got down to the beach and immediately began gathering up branches and twigs.

After a time Ethel said breathlessly, "We're wasting time, both collecting stuff. I'll make the sign, and you get the sticks."

Millie thought that sounded like a good idea and set about gathering branches and twigs of all sizes. When she couldn't hold any more, she went and threw them on the sand next to Ethel, who was diligently going about making the sign.

Millie didn't even stop to see what Ethel was writing as she hurried off to find more materials.

Millie was far away at the other end of the beach when she noticed Ethel now just standing still. She had stopped making the sign and was looking up to the sky.

Millie looked up too, in the same direction as Ethel, and could see something, just a dot, high up in the sky. When the thing went in front of the sun she had to blink, but it was rapidly getting bigger and bigger; whatever it was, it was drawing nearer to them by the minute.

Had the plan worked and they were being rescued?

Excited, Millie ran back across the beach towards Ethel and the sign. By the time she reached Ethel she could see what was coming down directly towards them: a police helicopter!

Ethel was jumping up and down, frantically waving her arms and shouting, "Help! Help! I'm over here!"

Millie wondered how they would both fit on the helicopter. It really was very small and there didn't seem much room. Then she noticed what Ethel had written with the branches and twigs:

HELP ME

"Ethel!" shouted Millie. "Why didn't you write 'Help *US*'? They could have sent something bigger to rescue us!"

"Sorry, Millie," replied Ethel. "I wasn't thinking. perhaps you should make another sign? I'm getting out of here; this rescue is for me."

As the helicopter circled above them it lowered a rope, which Ethel grabbed with both hands and it began to winch her up.

"Bye, Millie," she called down. "Say goodbye to the pirates for me, and good luck getting back. I almost feel bad about this," and off she went, gradually being lifted up closer to the hovering helicopter.

Above the noise of the helicopter Millie heard lots of shouting from behind her and knew what she would see when she turned: a horde of furious pirates charging towards her. They had realised the girls had escaped.

Millie was petrified that they were about to drag her back to the octopus cave, but in fact they raced straight past her as she dived behind a rock. They were chasing the helicopter!

One of the pirates threw his sword at the helicopter. The blade spun and twisted like a boomerang, but it wasn't aimed at the helicopter itself and instead hit the winch rope Ethel was hanging on and sliced right through it.

Ethel plummeted back towards the ground and the waiting pirates stretched out a blanket between them like a trampoline, which Ethel landed on, even bouncing a few times.

"Arrrrrghh," they shouted, high-fiving each other, rolled up the blanket trapping Ethel inside and carried her off.

Millie could hear Ethel screaming – "Millliiieeeee!!! Heellllpppp meeeeeee!!!" – but Millie had no intention of coming out from behind that rock. Especially as the helicopter was still hovering there.

She heard one of the pirates saying, "Thar was another girl. Where be she?"

Then she heard Hooky's voice. "Nope, don't think there was. You chaps must be mistaken. Definitely just the one."

And off they went, back to the all-seeing octopus.

Millie dashed out from behind the rock, back to the sign. The helicopter began to lower the rope again. Was it long enough now the pirates had cut it? No, not quite! Millie jumped with all her might but she couldn't reach it.

The helicopter came lower and lower, wind from the blades scattering sand (and the sign) everywhere.

Finally, with her biggest leap, Millie grabbed hold of the end of the rope and it began to winch her up. As she was pulled up to the helicopter she looked down but saw no sign of the pirates.

Then as she got ever higher Millie stopped looking down as she was afraid of heights.

When she was finally hauled up into the helicopter she could see it was indeed just a two-seater, with the pilot, a woman police officer, in the front seat. She looked familiar. Millie was sure she had seen her somewhere before.

"Hi!" she shouted above the noise as Millie clambered into the back seat. "I'm Officer White – we got your message and I was dispatched to help."

"The police can help in cyberspace?" shouted back Millie as the helicopter suddenly lurched forward, swept around the bay of the island and sped off out to sea.

"We can certainly try!" hollered back Officer White. "Most people don't let us know they are in trouble in cyberspace. You and your friend were very clever to ask for help."

"She's not my friend," shouted back Millie, who noticed they were now nearing land again. "She just tried to get herself rescued. She would have left me there with the pirates. Officer White, we have to go back to help the other people. Please!"

"We will Millie don't worry. This girl sounds like a terrible bully though," said Officer White as they crossed the shore and began their descent towards a building. "Have you told anyone else about her?"

"Not really," said Millie. "My friends in school know, but I haven't told a grown-up."

They landed on a big H in front of a building that Millie realised was a police station. It was very busy, with police cars whizzing in and out of the car park and more helicopters taking off and landing.

Officer White helped Millie out of their craft and led her into the building. As they walked down a long corridor, other police officers appeared at doorways and high-fived Officer White, whooping, hollering and shouting. "Great job, Officer White!"

They all seemed incredibly happy that Millie had been rescued. It seemed this entire police station was dedicated to helping people who had got into trouble in cyberspace!

Millie was led in through a door marked 'OFFICER WHITE UNIT' and the police officer pulled a Zablet from a drawer in her desk.

"Just as you got here, this will get you home," she said.

Millie reached out, but Officer White held it back for a moment and gave Millie a firm look.

"Promise me you'll tell your parents or a teacher about Ethel when you get back," she said.

Millie gulped. "Yes, Mrs … I mean, Officer White, I will. I'll tell my mother and father."

"Good," replied Officer White, and handed her the police Zablet.

"I can't help you with bullying at school – only if it becomes a problem in cyberspace – but other people can. Now I have to go back to that island with my team and arrest some very naughty pirates and a rather evil octopus."

"What about Ethel?" asked Millie.

"When we find her we'll send her back home too," said Officer White.

Sensing that Millie was worried that Ethel would have it in for her even more after this, Officer White added, "Don't worry, Millie. We'll wipe her memory. She won't remember a thing about any of this."

Millie turned on the Zablet, but then looked at Officer White who was busily preparing her pack for the mission. "What app do I open to get home?" she asked.

"Just press the Home button, silly," said Officer White, but not nastily, and she hurried out of the room.

Millie put her thumb on the Home button, closed her eyes, counted to ten and *POP!* she was back in her bedroom with her own Zablet on her lap.

After escaping the cyberspace pirates, Millie decided to leave the Zablet alone for a while. A few days later, on the walk home from school, Mum announced that they would be going to the farm for the rest of the afternoon as the weather was nice.

Millie needed cheering up as Ethel had been calling her names again, and she really liked it at the farm; there were lots of animals to see, plenty of activities to do and a big play area called the Fun Barn.

Harry was even more excited, and after a short drive they arrived at the entrance, which had a huge picture of a pig with "PORKY PIG FARM' written across his tummy. In the car park Millie noticed a big black car with enormous chrome wheels and dark tinted windows in the next parking space.

She recognised this as Ethel's mother's car.

Oh no – that meant Ethel was at the farm too. She was the last person Millie wanted to see.

Millie's mother got some pellets from the farm shop for the children to feed the rabbits by hand, and they were having a nice time doing so (although the one Millie was feeding did remind her a little of the pink rabbit who turned out to be a troll in Titter land) when the rabbits suddenly scattered off to the back of their pen. They peered out nervously from behind their hutch as a stone bounced off of the wall nearby.

"Ugly animals, and an ugly friend they have," said an all-too-familiar voice.

Millie turned to see Ethel pointing out the rabbits to the friend she was with, and she then threw another stone at them.

"That's horrible, Ethel," said Millie. "You shouldn't do that to little animals."

"Oh, shut up," Ethel sneered, "or I'll throw them at you instead."

Ethel and her friend were looking menacing, so Millie decided to move on.

As she trudged off to the Fun Barn she did wonder if she should tell Mum about Ethel and how horrible she was being. She had told Officer White she would, and telling her might make it all go away, but Millie felt ashamed that she couldn't deal with this on her own.

She should be able to.

Millie caught up with Harry and Mum and they went off into the Fun Barn to jump, climb, slide and swing, with more than a bit of shouting and screaming thrown in. It was a lot of fun and for a while Millie even forgot about Ethel.

That was until she was standing at the top of the biggest slide, waiting for Harry to finish sliding down and get out of the way at the bottom. As she was afraid of heights Millie was plucking up her courage when a hard shove sent her flying and she fell onto her front and went sliding down face first, just missing landing right on top of Harry.

Millie got quite a shock and was shaking. She looked back up the slide to see Ethel pointing and laughing at her.

"Haha! Look at silly Millie, fallen down the slide because she was so scared!" sneered Ethel at the top.

Millie couldn't believe Ethel could be so nasty and felt like crying, but she didn't want Ethel to see her that upset so she just ran off.

Mum was sitting nearby reading a book and hadn't seen what had happened, but Millie didn't want to tell her about it so asked if she had bought the Zablet out with them.

"Yes, Millie darling, it's in my bag. Are you getting a bit tired?" asked Mum, and gave her the Zablet.

When Millie nodded glumly Mum said "You can sit somewhere quiet with it if you like, but don't go too far away."

Millie took the Zablet and went to the wooden climbing pirate ship – very different to Hooky's ship. Underneath the ship was a playroom, which was quite dark inside as it was late in the day.

There was nobody in there so Millie went in and sat down on the floor with the Zablet resting on her crossed legs. Before she had even had a chance to turn it on it whistled at her.

She was trembling as she pressed the button – being bullied by Ethel was dreadful and Millie felt as if she just wanted to escape somewhere, anywhere.

She swiped through various apps and games before she saw "FaceSpace" which Mum and Dad and older children she knew used.

That sounded good. The FaceSpace icon was also glowing a bright white, almost as if it wanted Millie to press that and nothing else.

So Millie closed her eyes, laid her writing hand on the Zablet and started counting: One … two … three … nine … TEN!

When she opened her eyes she was standing in a street, a street in what seemed to be a very busy city.

Millie stood on the pavement as cars whizzed past in both directions. Buildings lined both sides of the road, buildings of many different shapes and sizes. There were big buildings, small buildings, narrow buildings, wide buildings, castle-shaped buildings, see-through buildings and Millie could even see a building that looked like a great big orange. There were shops and people hurrying everywhere; it really was hustle and bustle here in FaceSpace.

On the door of every building was a picture of a person, and Millie stopped at a small two-storey house and looked at a picture of a lady and what appeared to be her dog. A window on the top floor was flung open and the lady from the picture stuck her head out.

"Hello there," she shouted down. "Do you like my picture then?"

"Erm, yes, it's very nice," replied Millie, craning her neck.

"Oh, thank you." The lady beamed. "We can be friends then!"

Then the head promptly went back inside and Millie heard her shouting. "Oh, shut up, Roxy! SHUT UP! STOP IT! SHUT … UP!"

Millie realised the lady was shouting at a barking dog inside, probably the dog from the picture. It all sounded a bit too feisty, so Millie walked on. She wasn't sure she wanted to be friends here.

As Millie couldn't believe it: FaceSpace was real!

All of the buildings had pictures on their doors. Some of the bigger buildings had pictures on the windows too, usually of the same people as on the door but doing different things.

Millie stopped suddenly outside another two-storey house on the corner of this road and her mouth gaped open in surprise.

She looked at the face on the door, which was very familiar.

A green cap, wild orange curly hair … Millie tried to recall where she knew the face from, when the sound of a window being flung open made her look up again.

"Mills! I LIKE this! Epic! Like!" shouted a voice she recognised from Titter land.

Crackers!

The door opened and out dashed Crackers, who flung his arms out and gave Millie a huge hug.

"Mills! I don't believe it! What are you doing here? Come in! Come in!" he implored, so Millie followed him inside.

Crackers's house was very cosy, with pictures on mantelpieces, cupboards, walls and windowsills.

"Do you like my FaceSpace pad, Mills?" asked Crackers.

"I've been spending more time here since the trolls began to spoil Titter land."

"This is a house, not a pad, isn't it?" replied Millie, confused. "But I do like it, whatever you call it. This place is so big and busy."

"Everyone in FaceSpace has their own pad, Mills," explained Crackers. "I suppose it is like a house or a site, but you decorate it with your own pictures and videos to brighten the place up – and to put up a good image to impress your friends," he continued.

"Sometimes people even put a bit of news they might have on a banner across the front of their pad, if they have some good news to tell people, or even something to moan about."

He thumped down on the sofa and patted the spot next to him for Millie to sit.

"Yep. That's FaceSpace for you, a lot of real estate and space to put your things up. You know, pictures and stuff. Really quite fun, Mills. You should try looking up some people you know."

"How would I do that?" questioned Millie.

117

"You need to find your pad," said Crackers. "It's your space, and where you will find people you're friends with. It's that simple!"

Ten seconds after thumping down on the sofa the energetic Crackers leapt back up and marched off through another doorway. "I'll make us a snack in the kitchen, Millie. Sit tight. Or have a look around my pad if you like. I don't mind, seeing as we're friends."

Millie sat for a short time, thinking about the Ethel situation and what to do while listening to Crackers clattering and crashing around in the kitchen. She couldn't imagine what he was making for them.

On the walls around the pad (which Millie still preferred to think of as a house) Crackers had a single picture of every one of his friends. What's more, they were in alphabetical order.

Millie's eyes glanced across the pictures, row by row, to see if she recognised anyone. When she got to *M* she saw a familiar face: Madam Twinkle.

That's interesting, thought Millie; she hadn't known Crackers and Madam Twinkle were friends.

Millie continued scanning the rows of pictures. She looked past the fireplace, around the television and the chest of drawers, and finally behind the standing lamp she reached the Zs and she saw another face she recognised. Zoree the barn owl from Titter was there too, which was less of a surprise as Crackers and Zoree clearly knew each other and were friends.

"Let's scoff this down and go and find your pad," shouted Crackers as he walked back into the room carrying a tray of delicious-looking snacks.

After Millie and Crackers finished eating they set off in earnest. As they walked through a pretty green park Crackers explained, "Your pad will be in M District, Millie, and as we know we are leaving my pad which is in C District, we need to get from C to M – simples!"

They found themselves in streets beginning with D after they had crossed the park, then E and so on until they reached a street called Magic Street.

"Magic Street is the first street in M District," said Crackers. "We must be close now."

Magic Street was a very curious one, with the occupants of every pad seemingly either a witch, wizard, elf or some other mystical creature like a goblin or even a dragon.

Every so often there was a strange flickering at the window of one of the pads, or a peculiar bubbling noise emanated from a building, as if new spells and magic were being continually created and brewed.

One pad in particular was glowing bright blue from every window with a *pop-pop-pop-pop-pop-pop-pop-pop* sound that could continually be heard.

"Is the wizard who lives here making a powerful new spell, Crackers?" asked Millie.

"I'M A SORCERER, NOT A WIZARD!" boomed a voice from inside the house.

A surprised Millie whispered to Crackers, "What's the difference?"

He shrugged. Apparently Crackers didn't know *everything*.

Although it was very colourful and mysterious, Millie was pretty sure she didn't want to be friends with anyone on Magic Street.

"Millie's pad!" exclaimed Crackers. "I don't believe it, you're right next door to Magic Street – you lucky thing!"

Millie wasn't sure if that was lucky or not, but she was surprised to next see a nicely presented and tidy pad with a picture of her on the front door.

"This is your pad, Millie. As I said, everyone in FaceSpace has their own one," said Crackers. "Go in and take a look, why don't you?"

Millie turned the handle on the door, and finding it wasn't locked, she went straight in.

Crackers followed behind her. "You should set a password on your pad, Millie, to stop anyone getting in and messing about with your stuff, or even pretending to be you."

"I didn't know I could do that. Where do I set it?" asked Millie.

"Over here on this keypad by the door. Come and type it in," replied Crackers.

Millie thought for a second about what the password should be, but she was in a hurry as she wanted to look around her pad so she typed in something easy to remember – 'HARRY' - and pushed the green Set button.

The walls in Millie's pad were bare. Not a solitary picture.

"That's because you're new to FaceSpace and don't have any friends yet, Millie, but don't worry, we'll get that fixed that for you," explained Crackers while he fiddled with the lamp in a corner of the room.

He shook the lamp and tapped it hard, but the light wouldn't come on. Then Crackers noticed a small hole in the wall. "Aha! It's not plugged into the charger," he announced triumphantly, as if he had solved all of the world's problems.

But before Millie could stop him, Crackers poked his finger into the hole!

A *crack* and a *bang* and a lot of sparks threw Crackers across the room like a toy doll, where he thumped into a wall and lay motionless, smoke rising from his frazzled orange hair.

"Crackers! Crackers?! Oh dear. Are you OK?!" shouted Millie as she knelt down next to him.

"Crackers. Oh no, oh dear, oh no, what shall I do?" and she started to tremble, but just as she did from underneath that green cap she heard a faint giggling that got gradually louder before the crumpled heap that was her friend began to unravel.

Crackers sat up with a huge grin and more chuckling. "What on earth was that?" he asked.

"It's electricity, Crackers. It powers things like lamps when you plug them in and you definitely don't *ever* put your finger in a socket like that. You could have died!" said Millie.

Crackers looked thoughtful for a moment, his hair slightly singed.

"Elec tree cities … ?" he mused. "Hmmm. Didn't know you needed that – the lamp in my pad just worked so I didn't have to fiddle with it. But that was FANTASTIC! How much fun was that? The loud *bang* and then the flying! Absolutely brilliant! I'm going to have another go," he declared, but Millie grabbed his arm to stop him.

"Come on, Crackers – you're lucky not to be hurt really badly. You need to show me how to get some friends in FaceSpace."

Crackers looked disappointed as he appeared to have enjoyed the experience of hurtling across the room into a wall, but he got up, patted himself down and led Millie back out of the house.

"Just like we found your pad, Millie. We'll need to find your friends the same way, as you don't have any here yet," he said, as they stood outside Millie's house. "Who do you want to go and look for?"

"I suppose Nancy and Theo are my best friends. Can I look them up?" Millie asked.

"Course you can!" replied the ever-enthusiastic Crackers. "*N* for Nancy is next to *M* for Millie, so let's go this way; we can take a shortcut through Magic Street," and without waiting for Millie he began marching back the way they had come.

Millie wasn't ready to leave her pad just yet – she would have liked to decorate it a bit before her friends saw it, so she hung back, but suddenly a chill washed over her. You know that feeling you get when you're sure somebody is looking at you?

She looked around but couldn't see anyone; only a dim light at the top window of one quite creepy-looking house that went out as soon as she looked up. Millie dashed after Crackers.

As they continued along Magic Street Millie noticed a very familiar-looking shop on the other side of the road. It was Small and old-looking, with a fat little teddy bear in the window.

Millie read the sign: THE TWINKLE SECOND-HAND SHOP!

"Crackers, why is this shop in the M District? Twinkle begins with a T," stated Millie quite factually.

"Good question, Mills. The lady who owns this shop is called *Madam* Twinkle, which is why it's in the M District. I also think she likes being on Magic Street," explained Crackers.

"I've met Madam Twinkle before. Can we go and see her?" asked Millie.

"Sure," replied Crackers. "I'm friends with her too. Let's see if she's in. She does like to travel around a bit though, so she might not be."

They crossed the road (carefully) and Crackers strode up to the shop, cupped his hands around his eyes and peered in through the window.

"Hmmm, it doesn't look as if anyone is home."

He tried the door.

"No, it's locked, she must be out. We would never guess her password either."

Millie noticed the teddy. That same teddy Madam Twinkle had been cross with when they'd collected the Zablet was now facing them. He had a small mobile phone pressed to his ear.

"Crackers! That bear in the window – he didn't have a phone before, did he? Did you see?"

"No, Millie," said Crackers, distracted by another curiosity (a dancing sunflower) in the window display.

"No, he didn't have a phone, or no, you didn't see?" asked Millie, sensing she didn't have Crackers's full attention.

"Errmm, yes, whatever, Millie. How much do you think old Madam Twinkle would charge for those hair curlers there? Do you see them?" he asked. "My hair is a bit cranky after the elec-tree-city incident back at your pad."

The teddy now looked as if he was actually speaking into the phone.

"Come on, Crackers, let's go. That teddy is giving me the creeps," said Millie, and she set off.

Crackers finally noticed and ran after her. "Ah, Millie, you don't want to let enchanted teddy bears that belong to Madam Twinkle in a shop on Magic Street bother you too much. You can expect the unexpected here."

After a few minutes they reached N District, but they couldn't find Nancy's pad anywhere.

"I guess she's not in FaceSpace yet, Millie. Lots of people still aren't, as funny as that seems. Well, some people. A couple. Maybe just Nancy. Whatever. Come on, let's get a move on – we need to get you *some* FaceSpace friends."

The trekking about was getting very tiring, and as it was a warm day Millie and Crackers decided to rest on a patch of grass at the bottom of the last street in N District and make a plan about where to go next.

Suddenly they heard shouts of "ICE CREAM! ICE CREAM!" and saw a bright pink ice-cream van covered in flashing bulbs driving slowly by. The van stopped and the driver popped his head out of the window and waved at them.

He was a skinny little man with dark hair and a moustache and a pointy beard.

"ICE CREAM!" he shouted again.

Written on the van above the window was a sign which read:

BIG I SCREAM.

"I'd love an ice cream, Crackers. It's very hot and I'm hungry," stated Millie.

"Hmmm, be careful," said Crackers. "I don't know him. Do you? We don't even know how much it costs."

"FREE ICE CREAM!" boomed the voice.

Millie wasn't for turning down this offer now it was free, and she dashed over to the van.

"Why, hello there," said the small man in the van. "I'm the BIG I SCREAM man. BIS for short, if you're into acronyms."

Millie giggled. "Um, sorry, I don't mean to be rude, but you're not all that big, are you?"

He was smaller than Millie.

The BIS man didn't look offended at all so Millie continued, "I'd love an ice cream, please. Sorry, a BIG ice cream."

He quickly produced a cone from under the counter and then went to the back of the van, where he opened the lid of a large iron chest.

All manner of noises poured out of the chest. A *whoosh*, a sound like a firework … Crackers was sure he even heard a scream.

The inside of the chest was pulsating a luminous green, which made the whole inside of the van glow; even the BIS man himself took on a ghostly green aura.

Millie and Crackers, who had joined her, kept jumping up to try to look into the van to see what was going on in there.

Laughing as he did so, the BIS man dramatically plunged the cone down into the chest and it came back out with a scoop of delectable-looking minty-green ice cream.

He shuffled back to counter where they were waiting and held it out to Millie, who gratefully took it and, not forgetting her manners, said, "Thanks!"

She ran back to the grass where they had been sitting.

"Are you not having one, Crackers?" asked Millie as she slurped at the ice cream, which was truly delicious.

"Err, no, didn't really fancy it, Mills – there was something about the BIS man I didn't trust. I've never heard of him, for starters."

"Well, he seemed very nice *and* generous and this is amazing ice cream." Millie beamed as she carried on slurping away.

"Yeah that's good, but in FaceSpace, you know … well, people you *don't* know … It's really hard to tell if they are good people or not, Mills," said Crackers. "Since I've been here I've just learned to be a bit more suspicious of people and their motives – what do they want in return?"

Millie thought Crackers was being a little paranoid. She finished off the ice cream and wiped her mouth with the back of her hand. "Come on, Crackers, let's find me a friend in FaceSpace."

But as she spoke the words Millie realised her voice was different. It sounded a little bit deeper. More like her dad's than her mum's voice.

"Are you OK, Mills?" asked Crackers, who had noticed something too.

Now Millie noticed that Crackers was looking up at her. Was Crackers getting smaller?

"I'm fine, Crackers – but you're shrinking," boomed Millie, with a now even deeper voice.

"Errmmm, it's not me, Mills. Look around you."

Millie looked to her left. The trees by the patch of grass were now the same size as she was!

She looked to her right. Not only was she looking down on Crackers, she was looking down at the ice-cream van too. Millie had grown to the size of tree!

"Help, Crackers! I'm a giant! I don't want to be a giant!" she boomed. "And I'm scared of heights."

Crackers shouted at the BIG I SCREAM man. "What have you done? Why has my friend turned into a giant?"

A smile creased in the corners of the BIS man's mouth.

"What did you think *BIG I SCREAM* meant?" he shouted back.

"You have one of these, you get big, you scream. Or in her case, moan a lot in a big deep voice. I would have thought that was fairly obvious. You really should think a bit more about what you are accepting in FaceSpace, don't you know! Ho ho! Toodle-pip!"

And with that he jumped back into the driver's seat of the ice-cream van and screeched off.

Crackers peered up at Millie. "I'm sorry, Mills, I tried to warn you. You really can't trust anyone in FaceSpace if you haven't met them before in real life."

"Am I stuck like this forever?" sobbed Millie in a deep, booming voice, as she sat down on the grass, being careful not to squash Crackers in the process.

Even sitting down on the grass Millie was still much higher than Crackers, so he clambered up onto her foot, then climbed her shin and perched on her knee.

"You are REALLY big, Mills. Like the size of a house kind of big. I think you've stopped growing now though, which is good. Can I slide down your shin? You can't go home like this though – you wouldn't fit in your house. Unless you live in castle. Do you live in a castle? I'd love to live inside a real castle, especially a giant's one like in that story about Jack and, um … what was it?"

"Stop it, Crackers!" thundered Millie, looking very upset, and so loudly that Crackers nearly went sliding backwards off her knee.

"Sorry, Mills, I forgot this is probably quite upsetting to you," said Crackers more sympathetically. "I got quite used to odd things like this happening in Titter. The WOW Wizard was always turning things into all kinds of unusual shapes and whatnot. Once I spent a whole day as an orange-and-blue duck called Gerald," he reminisced. "I was never quite sure why he did it to me. I don't think he was even being particularly wicked that day – or wise, come to think of it – just testing out a new spell."

"How did you get back to normal then?" asked Millie. "Did the wizard change you back, or did the spell wear off?"

"Oh, neither of those," replied Crackers, gazing up at the giant Millie.

"He went missing, and as far as anyone knew I might have stayed as Gerald forever if he hadn't come back. Many in Titter land are completely different animals or beings to how they started out. So you can never be sure who someone really is or was."

"So what happened?" asked Millie again.

"Oh yes, well, fortunately, you see, I made a new friend who knew a few tricks and was especially skilled at reversal spells, which was a stroke of luck," explained Crackers.

"Who was that?" asked Millie hopefully. "Can they help us now?"

Crackers's eyes lit up and he slid down Millie's shin, onto her shoe. He landed on the grass and started jumping up and down in excitement.

"Of course!" he shouted joyously. "Stupid me for not thinking of it! It was Madam Twinkle!" he hollered. "Come on, Mills – let's go and see if she's back at the shop!"

They made their way back through N District towards the Ms (for *Madam* Twinkle, remember?). Crackers had to take six steps for every one of Millie's, so long were her legs.

After they had crossed a few more streets Crackers was completely out of breath.

"Stop a minute, Mills," he panted. "Please, I need a rest. Your legs are so long I can't keep up."

"Well, if I'm to be this big, Crackers, then we might as well make good use of it," said Millie, and picked Crackers up and plopped him on her right shoulder. "Let's go!"

They made much quicker progress now as Millie marched on with giant strides.

People in the street stopped and gawped; even birds hovered in the air to look Millie right in the face as she was as high as they were, and she sometimes had to swipe particularly curious ones out of the way.

Finally they crossed into M District and then, with Crackers barking directions from her shoulder, Millie marched on to Magic Street and up to Madam Twinkle's shop.

And what a commotion there was when they got there. There was a police car right outside and two police officers in conversation with … yes, it was Madam Twinkle!

The first policeman looked a little scared when he saw giant Millie stomping towards them with a tiny man on her shoulder.

Then the other one looked down at his notepad and then back at Millie. "She fits the description! *That* is the girl and her accomplice who tried to break into your shop! Arrest them!" he shouted.

"You arrest them, you're the police," shouted back the other policeman.

Millie was horrified and didn't know whether to flee.

Madam Twinkle also looked up angrily, preparing to confront the people who had apparently tried to break into her shop, but her eyes softened as she recognised the giant girl.

"It's Millie."

"Millie, eh? Millie the thief!" said the first policeman. "I'm going to arrest her right now. She's with her partner in crime too. Where can we get handcuffs big enough for her? Any hula-hoop rings left in the car, Bob?"

"I said it's *silly*, not Millie," Madam Twinkle corrected the policeman. "She doesn't fit the description at all!"

The now puzzled policeman scratched his chin and read what he had written down once again.

"*Weeellllll* … It says right 'ere in my notebook … shoulder-length brown hair, green school uniform …" he remarked.

The second policeman (Bob) chipped in. "Black shoes, button nose, it's her all right."

"You're missing one minor detail," said Madam Twinkle.

"And what, pray tell, is that?" asked the first policeman, who seemed to think he was the cleverer of the two.

"SHE'S A GIANT! Show me your notepad," demanded Madam Twinkle.

"Erm, OK, well, I suppose it does say a *little* girl," said the now extremely confused policeman.

"I suppose this isn't our suspect," he conceded.

"Well, there you have it," said Madam Twinkle. "You can be on your way, and you can also be sure I'll let you know if I see any suspicious *little* girls hanging about."

"OK then, Mrs Twinkle, I suppose we'll be off then," said the first policemen and they got back into their car and drove away.

"Madam Twinkle," stuttered Millie in her very deep voice, "we weren't trying to break into your shop, you know. We were just looking to see if you were open and we could come and see you."

"Yes, I know you're no kind of criminal, Millie," replied Madam Twinkle.

"You see, the teddy bear in my shop called me because he really is easily scared and a bit of a worrier. He saw you and, oh, is that Crackers up there on your shoulder? My goodness, so it is! Do put him down, my dear girl."

Millie gently lowered Crackers back down to the ground.

Madam Twinkle peered up and continued. "When Teddy called and said someone was trying to break in I was at the checkout in the curiosity supermarket, struggling with the self-service, you see. I couldn't get back quickly enough, so I told him to call the police. They were slow to arrive, so by the time I got back they had just got here." She shook her head.

"The break-in that wasn't is clearly the very least of our problems anyway, Millie."

"What is then?" boomed Millie.

"The biggest problem we have, my dear, and I do mean that in every sense of the word, is that you are the size of a house."

"Can you help Millie get back to her normal size, my dear Twinkle?" asked Crackers, his cheeky grin returning now that help was possibly at hand.

"Well, it just so happens that at the curiosity supermarket I bought the necessary ingredients for a zip-up spell," she replied. "So you're in luck."

Madam Twinkle went inside the shop and Crackers dashed in after her. Millie couldn't follow them because she couldn't fit through the door.

Standing on her own, Millie thought how incredible it was that she was outside the Twinkle Second-Hand Shop once more. And not only that, but looking down on it, which was especially strange.

She thought back to the evening when she had gone to the shop for the first time, to collect the Zablet with Mum, Dad and Harry, and suddenly she missed them and felt a long way from home.

"Hello there," came Madam Twinkle's voice.

Millie looked down, but nobody was there. She looked a little higher, and there was the mystical lady climbing out of a small door on the roof of the shop building, with a rope tied around her waist. The roof was at about the same height as Millie's waist.

Millie could see that just inside the open door Crackers was holding onto the other end of the rope.

"I need to sprinkle this zip-up dust all over you, Millie, to compress you back up," explained Madam Twinkle. "You're far too big for me to do that down there, so I need to be up here. Get as close to the building as you can and crouch down so I can sprinkle this over your head."

Millie did as she was instructed, and Madam Twinkle leaned out over her with Crackers resolutely holding onto the rope. So close was Millie's height to that of the building that Madam Twinkle could have stepped off of the roof onto her head, but she didn't and instead poured the glittery, silvery dust from a jar into a sieve and shook away.

When it was all gone Madam Twinkle shouted, "Pull me back in, Crackers, and let's see if this works."

At first Millie didn't feel any different.

"Can you feel anything happening, Mills?" called Crackers from the roof.

Millie shook her still very large head.

Then she began to feel a slight tingling, first in her head, which passed down her back, then her legs, before settling in her feet, which stayed tingly.

A bit like pins and needles.

"Anything yet?" asked Madam Twinkle.

Millie nodded. "Maybe a little tingle, but I'm still a giant. Why isn't it working?!"

Madam Twinkle and Crackers briefly looked concerned, but they needn't have.

POP!

Millie disappeared. Madam Twinkle and Crackers stood on the roof, staring at the sky where Millie had once been.

"She wasn't supposed to disappear," said a worried Madam Twinkle. "I really thought those were the ingredients for a zip-up spell."

Crackers looked distraught. "What do you mean, *disappear*, Twinkle?! Disappear where?!"

"It's OK, I'm down here," shouted a voice.

Madam Twinkle and Crackers peered over the edge of the roof, to see Millie brushing the zip-up dust from her hair and clothes. She was back to her normal size.

"Hold on, Mills," shouted Crackers excitedly. "We're coming back down."

Crackers and Madam Twinkle rushed back down the stairs into the shop and then out to Millie, who was stood exactly where she had been, staring up in bemusement.

"That really was very strange," she said. "I'm not sure I liked being that tall."

Madam Twinkle giggled. "Millie, my dear, I'm pleased you've started using the Zablet to come on these adventures. But we're going to have to teach you to be a bit more careful with who you trust in cyberspace. Step inside my shop and I'll show you."

They all went into the shop, the first time Millie had been in there since they collected the Zablet. It was just as she remembered, dark, musty, the shelves stacked with all manner of things of all shapes and sizes.

Madam Twinkle went behind the counter, on which sat a wonderfully ornate bronze and wooden cash register. She then disappeared through another door at the end of the shop, which slammed shut behind her.

"Hurry up, the pair of you," they heard her shout, and Crackers dashed ahead. He stopped and held the door ajar, then looked back at Millie.

"You coming, Mills?" he asked.

Millie thought about it for a moment. She did need to be more suspicious of people in FaceSpace. That was clear.

In fact she needed to be suspicious of people in the entire world inside the Zablet (or "cyberspace" as Madam Twinkle called it), but she knew Madam Twinkle, didn't she?

And Madam Twinkle *had* helped her and reversed the effects of the growing spell. Millie smiled and followed Crackers through the door.

They were gobsmacked when they saw what was on the other side. They were in what seemed to be an airport terminal. And it was huge! It didn't really make sense that such a huge building could be attached to the tiny shop. And it was so busy! And not just with people either.

There were elves. There were kings and queens. There were pixies. Farmers. Goblins. Postmen. Dwarves. Policemen and Policewomen. Troll families. Orcs. Wizards. Witches. And ordinary people too, all going this way and that, just like at a very busy airport.

"Welcome to the Be-Who-You-Want Port!" proclaimed Madam Twinkle, her arms thrust out wide.

"The what-who-you-what port?" asked Millie, completely baffled.

"Be-Who-You-Want, Millie!" said Madam Twinkle again. "Here you can simulate being anyone or doing something you always wanted to do. It's virtual reality, and my latest project!"

She pointed at the departures board. "Want to be a princess? Then take the flight to the fairy-tale kingdom. It's leaving in five minutes."

"How about an astronaut?" asked Crackers. "I always wanted to be one of those."

"Over there" Madam Twinkle pointed. "Join the astronaut group queuing for the flight for Cape Canaveral." (Ask your parents where that is.)

"Who are all the people in smart jackets and hats queuing over there?" asked Millie, pointing at a group of pristinely dressed men and women.

Some were wearing smart blue blazers with a winged golden crest on the pocket and stripes on the shoulders. Some were wearing an airline pilot's hat, others carrying theirs under their arm. Some were in old-looking brown leather hats, with goggles attached and jackets to match. Others still had diamond-white shirts on, without a single crease to be seen, and impeccably straight neckties.

"That's the pilots' group," said Madam Twinkle. "In that group you actually get to fly a plane around FaceSpace."

Millie thought that sounded like a lot of fun, and as if he could read her mind Crackers shouted, "That sounds super-cool! Can we go and join that queue?"

"Yes, I know most of the pilots in the group. Go for it, you two," replied Madam Twinkle. Off they went to join the group. At least Millie and Crackers did. Madam Twinkle held back and watched them.

As they joined the line of pilots, many in the queue turned round and doffed their hats to Millie and Crackers, which made them feel welcome and even more excited. When they reached the front of the queue a stern-looking lady sitting behind a counter looked them up and down. "Please go that way through the uniform converter to board your aircraft."

Millie thought the uniform converter looked exactly like the scanning machines you have to walk through at real airports, and when Crackers went through it beeped just like one too, but once on the other side Crackers was dressed in a pilot's uniform!

Next it was Millie's turn, and again it beeped (three times) and when she came out the other side she was also wearing a very smart pilot's uniform.

Millie's uniform was very neat, with a white shirt and pleated trousers. Crackers's consisted of a well-worn brown leather bomber jacket with a hat that had earflaps and goggles.

They went through another door and found themselves outside in front of two aeroplanes. It was easy to guess which one was whose.

Millie's was a huge passenger jet with lots of rows of seats inside, and Crackers's was a tatty old green plane with propellers on each wing.

They looked at each other a little nervously.

"Twinkle said it was safe, Mills. Let's go," said Crackers. He gave a cheeky wink and then almost fell up the ladder leading to the cockpit of his aircraft.

Millie's had a long, steep set of steps leading up to hers and when she had climbed them she too headed for the cockpit. There was nobody else in there.

Millie plopped herself down in the pilot's seat. In front of her was a big stick with a grip on it and a red button on which there was a label:

PRESS TO FLY

As Millie was debating whether or not to press it, the sight she saw next made her want to do so instantly.

Crackers was up, up and away and whizzing around in the sky in front of her.

"Millie! Whoooooohoooo! Can you hear me? They have radios in the planes! Over!"

Next to Millie was a radio on a curly wire. She picked it up and pressed the button on it and spoke into it.

"Yes, Crackers, I can hear you. I'm going to take off now. I'll see you in the sky! But how do I fly left or right?"

Then silence. Nothing.

Millie pressed the button and spoke again. "Crackers, did you hear me?"

"Yes. Over!" came back the reply.

"Why didn't you answer me?" asked Millie.

"You have to say over when you've finished saying your bit," came back the voice from the cockpit of the plane currently doing loop-the-loops in the sky in front of Millie. "And you didn't say over. Over!"

"Ahhh, OK, I get it now, Crackers. Over!" said Millie, and pressed the button on the stick.

The plane shot forward down the runway and gathered speed. Within seconds it soared up into the air.

Millie clutched the stick and pulled it left and the plane turned that way. When she pulled it right, it went that way. If she pulled it back towards her the plane went up, and when pushed forward it went down.

"That's it, Mills, you've got it! Over!" shouted Crackers on the radio, and with that they were off.

And what fun they had.

Millie soon had the hang of it and they flew all over FaceSpace, high above the city. They carried on beyond the city where there were fields beneath them, and on they went. They saw beaches below and then out across the sea they sped – every now and then Crackers would do a trick like a loop-the-loop in front of Millie's plane (which was bit less agile due to being so big, and therefore not so good for tricks).

But what fun it was to fly! Millie imagined she was taking a plane full of excited passengers on holiday, perhaps to somewhere like Mesalonia.

She picked up the radio. "Crackers, this is brilliant! I'm actually a real pilot!"

Silence. Then she remembered. "Over!"

Another voice – not Crackers's – came over the radio.: "Can the pilots please turn back now? You are leaving FaceSpace airspace and we are unable to watch you if you do."

Millie began to steer her plane round slowly in a wide arc, but as she was turning she noticed Crackers kept on shooting straight ahead.

"Crackers, we have to go back. Over," she shouted into the radio.

"Millie! I can't turn round – I can't change direction at all! I can't control it. I don't know what to do! Over!" came the crackly reply from a terrified-sounding Crackers. His voice was beginning to break up.

"I'll come after you. Over!" hollered Millie down the radio.

They were now flying in opposite directions and the distance between them was rapidly increasing.

Millie just made out Crackers's response. "No, don't, Millie. Something strange is happening. Go back and be safe – I'll be …"

Then came the sound of interference and crackling and Millie never even heard Crackers say "… OK, Mills. Fly safely. Over!"

A few minutes later Millie landed her plane safely back at the airport. A team of elves scrambled across the runway and connected the stairs to the plane and Millie disembarked.

She dashed back into the airport building and through the uniform converter so she was back in her normal clothes.

Millic rushed about desperately, looking for Madam Twinkle to tell her what had happened. People and creatures

141

were running about every which way, many looking very fraught and concerned, some in a blind panic.

"Millie! Millie! Over here," shouted Madam Twinkle above the noise.

Millie saw her waving and dodged and ducked her way through the crowds to reach her.

"Oh, Madam Twinkle, I don't know what happened to Crackers – it's terrible. He couldn't stop his plane and …" blurted Millie.

"Oh, my, it's worse than I thought," said Madam Twinkle gravely. "Everyone is panicking because there has been a sighting of a world-wide witch, the most wicked witch imaginable, Millie!" She continued. "A world-wide witch can appear anywhere, or be anyone. They will lie and deceive and trick you into being friends with them in cyberspace or even meeting them … And then they capture you."

Millie recalled how Crackers seemed to have been following something, as if he knew where he was going.

He *had* been tricked – that much was clear – and this really was a terrible situation.

Now, while all this was happening, back in the Fun Barn far, far away somebody was peering through a gap in the wall of the playroom where Millie had been.

That somebody had been spying on Millie, at first with interest and then with complete and utter astonishment as she was sucked into the screen of the Zablet and disappeared completely.

When Ethel could see there was nobody else about she crept into the playroom and saw the Zablet lying on the floor. Carefully she approached the Zablet, double-checking she was alone and that nobody was lurking in the shadows.

What was Millie up to? What had she been doing? And where was she now? All of this talk about magic had made Ethel quite curious, even if she thought Millie ridiculous.

Ethel sat down and pressed the big triangular button on the front of the Zablet and instantly the screen illuminated, lighting up her face in the darkness.

Ethel was delighted to find there was no password. Her big sister had a Zablet, and you had to type a password to do anything at all on it. Ethel had no idea what the password to that was; it had numbers and letters and maybe even some symbols. Nobody else in the family could use her Zablet because of that. Ethel hated her big sister.

Ethel saw the FaceSpace icon glowing and tapped on it.

ENTER PASSWORD

She thought about it.

She typed 'PASSWORD'.

WRONG PASSWORD. PLEASE TRY AGAIN.

She tried 'TYLER' (Millie's surname).

WRONG PASSWORD. PLEASE TRY AGAIN.

Ethel wondered about Millie's annoying little brother. What was his name? Tommy? Mickey? Then she remembered hearing Millie calling down to him from the top of the slide, and she typed 'HARRY'.

FaceSpace opened up immediately and as Ethel swiped the screen, looking at pictures and details of people she didn't recognise, her jaw dropped open when she got to a picture of Millie with a tiny little man with wild cranky hair, whom if Ethel didn't know better she would say looked rather like a pixie.

Ethel swiped some more and stopped immediately when she saw another amazing picture. This time it was of Millie next to a building which on its own wouldn't have been very interesting – but in this picture Millie was bigger than the building itself!

And what's more, two much smaller people were on the roof of the building, apparently talking to her: the odd-looking little man and a lady who looked like a gypsy fortune-teller.

Already stunned by quite simply the most bizarre set of pictures she had ever seen, what she saw next would have made Ethel fall over, had she not already been sitting on the floor. A video of Millie Tyler – from her class, in her school, Silly Millie – flying an aeroplane!

There she was sitting in the pilot's seat, with a pilot's hat and a pilot's uniform, her hands on the controls, with a big beaming smile, and all that could be seen through the window was clouds. She was turning the plane this way and that and looked as if she was having a great time.

This displeased Ethel greatly and she was desperate to find out more about what exactly was going on. She thought back to what Millie had been doing when she was spying on her through the crack in the wall.

She had seen Millie put her hand on the screen and close her eyes. She hadn't been able to quite hear what Millie had been saying, but Ethel thought it looked as if she had been counting.

This is absolutely ludicrous, thought Ethel, but nobody was around to see her, so she placed her hand on the screen and closed her eyes tightly.

She started counting: "One … two … three … four … five …"

This was idiotic. How long did she have to count for?

"… six … seven … eight … nine …"

"Millie! Where are you?!"

The shout from outside snapped Ethel's concentration and stopped her counting.

It was Millie's annoying little brother, obviously trying to find her like Ethel was, only for different reasons. He was just outside the playroom, walking around and looking in.

What did that little brat want?

Ethel slipped into the shadows and turned the Zablet over so it was dark inside the playroom; she held her breath and was quieter than a mouse.

Harry slipped his head around the door. "Millie? Are you in here?" he said softly, mainly to himself as he could see there was no one there. Nothing.

"No, you aren't," he muttered and left.

Ethel breathed out, turned the Zablet over and put her hand on the screen once more. She closed her eyes again.

"… TEN!"

When Ethel opened her eyes again she wasn't in the playroom any more.

She wasn't even in the Fun Barn.

Ethel was on the corner of a street she didn't recognise. Definitely not a street in their village, this was a busy main road, with houses and buildings of all shapes and sizes. It felt like it was part of a busy mishmash of a city, judging by the people rushing about and cars speeding in all directions.

Ethel read the sign immediately above her on the side of a house and things became even more interesting:

MAGIC STREET.

Crackers was scared. He wasn't usually scared or easily scared, but right now he was. Scared with a capital S.

What he had been following in his plane – or what he *thought* he had been following – was his old friend the WOW Wizard.

The wizard had appeared in front of Crackers's plane riding an incredible flying bicycle. From the saddle of the multicoloured BMX-style bike the wizard had waved and beckoned Crackers to follow.

Over the radio the WOW Wizard spoke to him. "Come on, Crackers! Follow meeeee!"

So Crackers did.

He hadn't stopped to think that he wasn't even friends with the WOW Wizard on FaceSpace. In fact, the WOW Wizard had said many times that he would never leave Titter in case it fell to the trolls.

As they shot off even further ahead of Millie's plane, Crackers realised he couldn't turn his plane right or left any more. The plane was flying straight on by itself.

It was about then that the instruction to turn back came to them over the radio, but it was too late; Crackers was locked in to following the WOW Wizard.

And as he drew closer the WOW Wizard slowly began to change shape, and when he finished morphing Crackers could now see as clear as day that he hadn't been following the WOW Wizard at all but a witch!

And not a witch on a broomstick either – this one was riding a hoverboard!

The witch began to descend in circles, round and round and the plane obediently followed. Crackers desperately rattled the steering stick, but a blue light in the cockpit blinked repeatedly above a sign that said 'AUTO-PILOT'. It was no use, it seemed to be under her control.

They landed in a field. Crackers was paralysed – at first he thought with fear, until he realised that he actually couldn't move a muscle because of a spell the witch had cast on him.

The witch strode forward to his plane with her hoverboard under her arm, but when she saw Crackers she was aghast!

"I wanted the girl!" she roared. "Not some scruffy little pixie!"

Crackers couldn't even speak to tell her he wasn't a pixie, he was just small.

"I WANT THAT ZABLET!" screamed the witch, so loudly that Crackers's ears actually buzzed a little.

With that she withdrew a shiny white phone from her cloak. It had *i-magic* written across the back.

She pointed it at Crackers and chanted:

You foolish pixie,
You should have known,
I wasn't your friendly Wizard,
But a witch with an i-magic phone!
I'll put you in my dungeon,
With walls made of granite,
Until I capture that girl
And her enchanted Zablet!

A flash of light shot from the phone and wrapped itself around Crackers. Everything went dark, and he felt himself being lifted away but couldn't see a thing.

The next he know, he was in a cold, dark and very small room and he could barely see a thing in there either.

The walls and floor were made of smooth black shiny granite, just as the witch had said. A chink of light shone through one tiny gap at the top of the dungeon, where the ceiling met the wall.

Crackers sat down on the only piece of furniture, a small sofa, and put his head in his hands and sighed deeply.

Was Millie safe? Why did the witch want the Zablet? Did Madam Twinkle know this witch was after Millie and the Zablet?

And then the biggest question of all.

Why, oh why, had he *ever* put trust in somebody's identity in the cyber world?

Madam Twinkle had summoned help from all of the cyber-folk at the be-what-you-want port.

The pilots, shocked at what had happened to someone in their group, commandeered every plane at their disposal and scattered across the skies of FaceSpace to search for Crackers.

The kings and queens sent a squadron of dragons back from the fairy-tale kingdom. They would be very useful when it got dark, illuminating the sky with their flames.

The astronauts sent messages up to their colleagues aboard satellites in orbit, asking them to report back if they noticed anything at all unusual in FaceSpace airspace.

The pilot leader was the first to report back, and his voice crackled over the radio. "Madam Twinkle, this is squadron leader Foxy Albatross, do you read me? Over."

"Have you found the pixie yet?" asked Madam Twinkle.

Silence …

Millie coughed to get her attention and explained politely. "You have to say 'OVER' when you're finished, Madam Twinkle, or they don't know it's their turn to talk."

"Ah yes, right you are," she replied. "To tell the truth, these walkie-talkie radios are a bit old-fashioned for me. I prefer apps and email and Zablets. Not these crackly old antiques."

Nevertheless she shouted back down the radio "Over!"

"No," came back the response. "Over."

Madam Twinkle and Millie looked hopefully at the kings and queens, hoping they might have had news back from the dragon squadron, but they shook their heads. Nothing at all.

The astronauts hadn't had any word from high up in space either.

Just where had that witch taken Crackers?

That was exactly what Crackers wanted to know. He was stuck in a pokey dark dungeon with no way out. Even the ceiling wasn't very high, adding to the sense of claustrophobia.

Then Crackers had a thought.

If he tipped up the sofa to stand on its side and climbed up that and then stood on top of it, he just might be able to see out through that crack and get some idea of where he was being kept captive.

Tipping it up was quite easy, but climbing up not so.

He fell off a couple of times and the sofa tipped over once, but eventually Crackers managed to balance precariously on the upturned sofa and push his face right up to the thin gap between the wall and ceiling.

He could make out cars whizzing by and footsteps overhead, so he could tell he was underground, but no clues as to his whereabouts.

Then Crackers noticed a reflection in the door of a car that had stopped. He could make out some words. It was a road sign!

He had to squint very hard to make it out and think very hard to decipher the mirror writing, but when he finally did his heart jumped and he almost fell off the sofa again.

The sign read 'MAGIC STREET'!

Crackers was being held in a dungeon right under someone's house in Magic Street. I can't be far from Madam Twinkle's shop at all, he thought!

Although there was a risking that the witch might be nearby, he started shouting through the gap: "Milliieeeee! Madam Twiiiinkkkllle! Heeeeelllllllppppp!"

Nearby a curious soul heard his muffled shouting coming from somewhere a short distance away. In fact, the sound seemed to be coming from a creepy-looking house, or to be more precise, from underneath it.

"HMMMMPHHH! HMMMPPPPH! MMMMM TTTWWWL!" – accompanied by a bit of thumping – was all Ethel could make out as she approached the source of the noise to investigate.

Crackers could see a shadow through the gap and knew somebody was very near.

If only he could get a message out!

He checked the pockets of his pilot's jacket – and had a stroke of luck at last!

A notepad and pencil were in the top-left pocket. Crackers pulled them out and frantically began to scribble the following message:

HELLO. IF YOU READ THIS NOTE, PLEASE TELL MILLIE AND MADAM TWINKLE! IT'S ME, CRACKERS, AND I'M TRAPPED HERE UNDERGROUND! PLEASE HELP ME. I KNOW YOU'RE NOT FAR AWAY!

If you think Ethel was surprised when a piece of paper began to appear from a crack in the ground, imagine her surprise when she read what written was on it. So Millie was nearby!

Harry hadn't much luck tracking down Millie in the Fun Barn. He was just about to go back and tell Mum he couldn't find her anywhere when he spotted something glowing inside that playroom under the pirate ship.

He peeked back around the door and this time saw Millie's Zablet, lying on the floor and illuminated. Funny, he thought, he hadn't seen a glow earlier.

He was starting to get worried. Where was Millie?

Had she gone on another adventure? Harry went into the playroom, picked up the Zablet and tapped the triangle button.

The FaceSpace icon was flashing manically, this time it was burning red. It simply *had* to be pressed.

ENTER PASSWORD

This was a blow. Harry really couldn't spell many words at all yet.

In fact the only word he could spell consistently correctly was his own name, so he typed it and would you believe it? FaceSpace opened up.

There were pictures of Millie doing all manner of things. Harry could not believe what he was seeing!

Millie flying a plane, Millie as tall as a house … it was all a bit much for Harry's young mind to take in.

Then there were pictures of that horrid bully Ethel, next to a sign that read 'MAGIC STREET'. Harry was better at reading than he was at spelling.

The last picture showed a little chap with scruffy orange hair, apparently called Crackers, whom it seemed was a friend of Millie's. His location was tagged "Trapped in a dungeon on MAGIC STREET."

What was Harry to do? He knew Ethel wasn't to be trusted, and this Crackers chap looked very distraught.

Harry thought about the adventure he and Millie had had to Mesalonia – how did they do that? Did they close their eyes and count? Hadn't they done something with their hand?

Harry put his (non-writing) hand on the screen and counted. When he got to twenty (which was as high as he could count) and nothing happened, he looked at the screen again. The Zablet whistled and the picture of Crackers flashed, as if to draw Harry's attention back to his plight, like it was trying to tell him something.

At the bottom of the screen was a box that said above it:

SEND A MESSAGE

"Great idea, Zablet! I can send a message to someone to help," said Harry out loud.

Harry tapped on the box and moved down the names until he found Millie. He tapped on her name and another box appeared for him to type a message into.

He was only just learning writing and spelling, but Harry knew he had to get a message to Millie to let her know Crackers was trapped.

So this is what he typed:

MILLIE (He could spell Millie's name too). CRACKERS IZ TRAPED. IN A DUNJEN. IN MAJIK STRET. YU NEAD TO HELP HIM.

He pressed Send.

Madam Twinkle and Millie had just got back through the door from the be-what-you-want-port into the shop.

"I'll send messages out to some more of my friends to find out if they have seen anything, or have any idea of where our little friend could be," said Madam Twinkle.

She began to rummage and rustle around on the shelves, discarding books and figurines. A cloud of dust enveloped her as she pulled out one thing and put it back, only to pull out something else equally useless.

Millie stood watching her, not knowing what to do to help, when she heard a buzzing noise.

"Madam Twinkle," she shouted above the clattering.

"What, my dear?" responded the busy lady.

"I thought I heard a buzzing noise coming from over there," said Millie, pointing to the desk with the antique cash register.

"Probably wasps," replied Madam Twinkle. "Don't open any drawers, dear. There was a nest here last summer – a terrible business was that."

Then the buzzing again.

"Errm, it doesn't sound like wasps, Madam Twinkle," said Millie.

She had heard a noise like that before, when her mum or dad had been sent a message on their phones.

"It sounds like a phone vibrating," she shouted, just as a porcelain goblin smashed on the floor, making Madam Twinkle jump with fright and then curse loudly.

Madam Twinkle stopped what she was doing and ordered a small round robotic vacuum cleaner to whizz across the room and clean up the mess. Then she looked at Millie as if an idea had struck and began to pat her pockets.

"My phone!" she exclaimed. "It's in the drawer."

She bounded over to where Millie was standing by the desk and looked quizzically at the drawers, of which there were three.

"I can't remember which drawer I put my phone in," she said. "One drawer definitely has a wasp's nest in it. Definitely. Most people poison them or remove them some other way, but I let them bee."

Madam Twinkle looked at Millie. "Joke. Geddit?" she asked.

"No, I don't. Sorry," replied Millie.

"It was a spell joke, Millie," said a now amused Madam Twinkle. "They're wasps, but I *let them bee."*

Millie stared open-mouthed at Madam Twinkle, not knowing what on earth she was talking about.

"I turned them into bees, Millie, much better-natured than wasps. See? I *LET THEM BEE*. I think there is even a queen in there," she explained. "Anyway, we still don't want to disturb them – that could turn nasty."

"So which drawer are they in?" asked Millie. "We don't want to open that one up."

157

"Precisely," said Madam Twinkle. "And I don't know. So you choose, Millie. I'm always making bad decisions – like going to the be-what-you-want port."

Millie looked at the drawers. She thought the top drawer of the three was the most likely drawer a person would put a phone in; it was easier to retrieve. She took a deep breath, put her hand on the handle and was just about to pull it when … *BUZZZZ … BUZZZZ … BUZZZZ …*

The buzzing noise she had heard was coming from the bottom drawer!

Millie snatched back her hand. She moved it to the bottom drawer instead and gently creaked it open, ever so slightly at first, tense and wincing as she did so.

But she soon saw a glowing object inside. Madam Twinkle's phone!

"And to think I nearly opened the top drawer," said Millie, handing the phone to Madam Twinkle, who was standing there beaming with pride.

"I knew you would make the right choice, Millie."

Madam Twinkle frantically tapped away at the phone, then looked at Millie in alarm her eyes wide. "It's a message from that boy who came to the shop with you the first time," said Madam Twinkle. "The boy Teddy Bear keeps talking about."

"Harry?" asked Millie, ever more puzzled.

"Yes, that's him," said Madam Twinkle, showing Millie the phone. "It's for you."

Millie's heart sank. Harry wasn't here in FaceSpace as well, was he?

"He's in the real world, don't worry," Madam Twinkle reassured her, reading Millie's face and her concern.

She continued. "The message says … 'Crackers is traped.' What does that mean? What is *traped*?"

"Let me see the message," said Millie, and grabbed the phone. She was used to reading Harry's spelling.

"Madam Twinkle, it says … and I don't know how he knows … but it says … Crackers is *trapped in a dungeon right here* in Magic Street and we have to help him!"

Madam Twinkle went back to the shelves and even more furiously than before began taking off one thing after another. All manner of objects crashed to the floor, but it didn't seem to matter; Madam Twinkle was determined to find something important.

Suddenly she announced, "Here it is!"

She held aloft a shiny silver orb.

"My Cyber-Ball!"

"What does it do?" asked Millie.

"This, my dear, is my Cyber-Ball. It's a near-range finder," explained Madam Twinkle triumphantly.

"It's a bit like a crystal ball, but with a high-definition picture. *If* Crackers is nearby, this will tell us exactly where, rather than just giving us a vague idea like those old-fashioned misty crystal balls."

Madam Twinkle placed the Cyber-Ball on the desk and rubbed it with her hand.

She frowned as some words slowly formed on the ball.

"NO SIGNAL."

"Arrrgghhh!" cried Madam Twinkle. "That's why I rarely use it – the darn thing never works when you need it most!"

She gave it a hard tap, but still the same words were displayed. Madam Twinkle picked up the Cyber-Ball and went over to the window.

"It should work better here," she said, sounding unsure, and rubbed it again.

This time the mists swirled and then an outline of a person appeared. A small person with scruffy curly orange hair. Crackers!

"He is very near," said Madam Twinkle. "In fact, out of the shop, turn right and walk fifty paces."

"Quick, let's go," implored Millie.

Out of the shop they went and marched along Magic Street, following the directions the Cyber-Ball was giving them.

Ethel saw Millie and a strange lady holding a peculiar round object with outstretched arms walking towards her. Before they saw her, she ducked down behind a car. Typical odd Millie, she thought, and who was this nut she was with?

Ethel watched as Millie and the weird lady stopped outside the creepy-looking house and looked down at exactly the same bit of pavement where the piece of paper with the message had popped out from. How did they know about this?

Madam Twinkle rubbed the Cyber-Ball, and once again Crackers's image appeared, sitting with his head in his hands, clearly sobbing.

"Now watch this," said Madam Twinkle, and winked at Millie. "If I press this button, tucked away underneath the ball, then he should be able to hear us."

Millie thought it sounded ideal if they could talk to Crackers and ask him secretly where he was and how they could help.

Madam Twinkle pressed the button and spoke.

'HELLO, CRACKERS! IT'S TWINKLE AND MILLIE – CAN YOU HEAR US? WHERE ARE YOU?'

The sound bellowed out of the Cyber-Ball and people stopped in the street to look. Madam Twinkle's voice bounced off of the walls, hit the trees and drowned out the noise of cars driving past. It was as loud as if she'd been using a loudhailer, and *everybody* must have heard.

"Madam Twinkle," whispered a concerned Millie, "the entire district must have heard that. I thought it was supposed to be private between us and Crackers. What if the witch heard?"

"Oh, I didn't say that, Millie." Madam Twinkle chuckled. "It was an announcement, a broadcast. Anybody nearby who was listening would have heard it."

"Yes, and anybody *not* nearby and *not* listening as well." Millie frowned.

Crackers had indeed heard them, and quickly lifted the sofa back up on its end, clambered up onto it and started shouting through the crack.

"Millie! Madam Twinkle! I'm trapped underground here. Look!"

Millie and Madam Twinkle heard the muffled shouting and then saw a piece of paper being pushed through a small gap between two of the paving stones.

I'M UNDER HERE! THERE IS A SECRET DOOR IN THE TRUNK OF THE TREE AT THE BACK OF THE HOUSE. THE WITCH BROUGHT ME DOWN HERE THAT WAY.

HELP!

Madam Twinkle knocked on the front door of the house, but there was no answer.

"Good, the witch isn't here," she said to Millie. "Let's see if we can find this tree with the secret door."

The entrance to the ramshackle garden was through a creaky, hanging gate. The fence was broken in many places, and everything was overgrown and hostile-looking, with thorns and spiky plants in abundance.

As soon as Millie and Madam Twinkle disappeared from view behind the house, Ethel crept out and picked up the note from the floor (which Millie had dropped by mistake – she wasn't a litterbug) and read it. She crept quietly into the garden, staying out of sight but watching their every move.

163

Millie ran to the tree Crackers must have meant, but could see no door, so she looked despairingly at Madam Twinkle.

"You'll have to tap around the trunk until it sounds hollow," explained Madam Twinkle, and started tapping away.

Firstly there was little noise as they knocked on solid wood, but suddenly there was a more distinct knocking noise when Madam Twinkle tapped one particular section.

"It's protected by a spell," she said, looking concerned. "I'll have to go back to the shop to get the bits I need for an unlocking spell. You stay here and keep watch, Millie. If the witch does return, hide."

Millie was scared but put on a brave face. "OK, but please hurry."

Madam Twinkle nodded, turned and hurried off.

She was so quick in fact that Ethel had to throw herself behind a wheelie bin to stay out of sight. It smelled repugnant and was sticky, slimy and extremely unpleasant. Millie Tyler was going to pay for this.

Millie kept an anxious lookout for any sign of the witch returning. She looked up in the sky too, but all remained quiet. Then she noticed a small rock on the floor, out of keeping with everything else around the garden; it looked as if someone had put it there deliberately.

She nervously looked around again, before picking up the rock. What had drawn her attention was not the rock itself, but what was underneath it: a small yellow piece of paper on the ground, like a reminder note.

Millie picked up the paper and read what was written on it.

THE PASSWORD IS KNOCKITY KNOCK KNOCK.

Millie was very surprised that a cunning, evil witch would be so silly as to leave a piece of paper with a password on lying around right next to the tree.

She held the note and read it out, in the direction Madam Twinkle had said the secret door was.

"The password is … Knockity Knock Knock," she announced.

The door swung right open. Lights came on inside, illuminating the steps that led down, down to where she hoped she would find Crackers.

Cautiously Millie crept in through the door and slowly down the dark, damp stairs. A constant *drip-drip-drip* noise put her on edge as she descended; it made the place sound spooky. After ten or so winding steps she came to a corridor lit only by very dull lamps. At the end of the corridor was a large wooden door with a padlock.

Millie crept to the door and tapped on it. "Crackers?" she whispered. "Are you in there?"

She heard hurried footsteps and then the voice she had hoped to hear.

Crackers shouted through the door. "Mills! You've come to rescue me! Oh, I knew you would! Please open the door and get me out of this horrible place!"

"I can't," whispered back Millie. "It's locked with a padlock."

She examined the padlock. When she turned it over she found a kcy taped to the back

This witch may be very powerful but she was NOT very smart at guarding what she wanted to keep, that was for certain.

The key came away easily and Millie inserted in the padlock and turned it. It was rusty and needed a bit of hard twist, but eventually it popped open and Millie removed it, then threw open the door to be met by an ecstatic Crackers.

"Mills! I knew you would come! Where is Madam Twinkle? Did you do this on your own? That is *soooo* brave. I don't think I could do something like that on my own I—"

It was always difficult to stop Crackers talking, but this time Millie interrupted. "Madam Twinkle helped me most of the way, but has gone back to the shop to get the ingredients for a spell to open the secret door in the tree. But I didn't need it as I found the password on the ground – the witch was really silly leaving it just lying around like that."

Another voice stopped them.

"Not as stupid as you, Millie Tyler," cackled the voice, and as they both turned to see who it was, the door slammed shut and they heard the padlock being closed again on the outside, this time locking both Crackers and Millie in the dungeon.

Crackers looked terrified. "It's the witch come back to turn me into a worm," he screamed.

"It's not the witch – I know that voice," said Millie solemnly.

"That's right, Millie dear," replied the voice sarcastically from the other side of the door. "It's your best friend in all the world, Ethel, come to let you know you can't escape me WHEREVER YOU TRY TO HIDE. At school or in this world. Especially when you are stupid enough to leave your Zablet lying around."

"I don't know what I'll do with you yet," said Ethel through the door, sounding very pleased with herself. "I might just leave you here forever, stuck in a tiny cell with your scruffy little friend," she mocked. "Or maybe I'll try and contact the witch and let her know I've trapped you here and I have the key. Perhaps I can trade you and the Zablet for a magic spell, one that I could take back to school, to turn the teachers into frogs."

Ethel was enjoying scheming out loud.

Millie and Crackers heard Ethel's footsteps going back down the corridor and up the staircase and Millie banged on the door with her fists.

"Ethel! What are you doing?! Stop it! Let us out now!" she shouted, but there was only silence.

Crackers just stood there staring at the door, open-mouthed. "I was free, Mills. Free."

He looked as if he was going to cry.

"And now we're *both* trapped. This is terrible. Who was that and why does she hate you so much?"

"That is Ethel Morgan," replied Millie despondently. "She bullies me and I don't know why."

"Some people are just bullies, plain and simple," said Crackers sympathetically, looking less sorry for himself now and more concerned for Millie.

"When I was young there was another child at Magic Cyber School called Isas," explained Crackers. "He was so mean to me, and I could never work out why.

"When we were practising spells he would stand directly in front of mine as I cast it, so he got turned into a mouse or a caterpillar or a horse or a … you get the idea. Then he would squeak or wiggle or neigh to the teacher to say I had cast the spell on him deliberately, so I got into trouble. Other times when I was reading quietly on a toadstool, he would creep up behind and push me off for no reason."

"That is *just* what Ethel is like," exclaimed Millie angrily. "How did you stop him?"

"In the end I told my dad," said Crackers. "He came to the school and had a quiet word with our teacher."

"Did that work?" asked Millie. "Did Isas stop bullying you?"

"No," said Crackers, and Millie's heart sank. "Well, not at first anyway." He carried on. "So I told my mum, and she has a stronger way with words than my dad. Mum went to the school for *another* few words, and eventually they took away Isas's magic as a punishment and put him in a different class so we weren't together. Once I was out of sight, he just seemed to forget about me." He sighed. "We're in a right pickle now though, Mills."

Back in the playroom, Harry was watching developments with horror. Now Millie was trapped and it was his fault!

He decided to send another message. This time to the teddy bear, whom he could also see on FaceSpace.

HELLO TEDDY BER. IM NOT SHOR IF U MEMBER ME BUT IM THE SAME BOY U WERE LOKIN AT IN THE

SHOP. MY SISTA IS TRAPED IN A DUNJEN AND NEADS YOUR HELP. I DON'T KNOW WAT TO DO.

Madam Twinkle was frantically rummaging in drawers, on shelves, in cupboards. In fact anywhere there might actually be anything useful.

"Drat my ingredient-filing system," she complained. "I can't find anything."

Her attention was caught by something moving in the shop. Teddy Bear had jumped down from the window and was walking towards her.

Madam Twinkle picked him up. "What is it, Teddy? You really are supposed to stay in that window in case somebody walks by who might want to buy you."

Teddy Bear held his phone up to show Madam Twinkle, and she read the screen with the FaceSpace message from Harry.

She looked up wide-eyed in horror. "Teddy, we have to go!"

While Madam Twinkle was running back down Magic Street, clutching Teddy in one arm and a book of spells in the other, her pockets stuffed full with spell ingredients, Ethel was using her own phone (her parents had given her one for Christmas and she used FaceSpace) to search for the witch.

She found Millie's FaceSpace pad and then went to her list of "friends". She scrolled through the short list – Crackers, Madam Twinkle, the BIS man – and then stopped on what Ethel thought must be her.

Wearing a black leather jacket, black skirt and boots, this wasn't a traditional-looking witch from children's books, but the crooked, pointed hat and the name – World-Wide Witch – made Ethel sure that it must be her.

The witch was on the list as a recently added friend of Millie's. Fantastic, thought Ethel. I can message her with my offer …

Ethel tapped the picture of the witch with her finger but what happened next surprised even her.

"Ouch," moaned a voice behind her, and Ethel turned to see the furious-looking witch towering above her.

"Who tapped me on my hat?" she demanded. "Was it you, little brat? You've crumpled it."

Suddenly Ethel wondered if this was such a good idea and was going to deny it, when the witch snatched the phone from her hands and read the screen.

"Why have you contacted me?" she blared.

Ethel trembled from her hair to her toes. "Um … Mrs Witch … I'm terribly sorry …" she stammered, "but I have something I think you want."

Ethel had to think fast. The witch *already* had Crackers trapped, so Ethel had to make her think she had helped in some way. "I've trapped someone else in your dungeon that I think you wanted very much," she said, a sly smile returning.

"Tell me more. Quickly," said the witch, now less interested in intimidating Ethel and more in listening to what she had to say.

Ethel took a deep breath and blurted it out. "I've trapped Millie Tyler in your dungeon. With my help, her enchanted Zablet can be yours – forever!"

Madam Twinkle crouched down out of sight, watching the witch and her new accomplice from precisely the same spot that Ethel had spied on Millie. As they descended back into the tree she fretted. "Oh dear, this is quite terrible. What am I going to do about this?"

Teddy Bear tapped Madam Twinkle on the knee (he was about knee high when standing on the ground) and showed her his phone.

Madam Twinkle read the screen. "A recipe for a banishment spell! Well done, Teddy!" she praised him. "But do I have the right ingredients?"

Madam Twinkle began to turn out her pockets. "Chewing gum chewed by a midget unicorn. Check!

"A pickled-onion Giant Gulp crisp. Check!

"A Yeti each yogurt. Check!

"A Mortar and Pestle?" said Madam Twinkle despairingly. "That was too heavy to bring. How will we grind it all together?"

Teddy pointed at the witch's roll-along suitcase left by the tree. Madam Twinkle's eyes lit up once again. "Oh, well done, Teddy, you are on fire today. I really may have to think twice about selling you!"

They crept carefully towards the suitcase, wanting to be sure the witch wasn't about to return.

Madam Twinkle opened the suitcase and rifled through the contents before she found exactly what they needed at the very bottom, an ingredient-grinding mortar and pestle.

Meanwhile, down below, Millie and Crackers heard footsteps approaching.

"Oooohhhh, Millieeeeee …" said an all-too-familiar mocking voice from the other side of the locked door. "I've brought somebody to see you, a new friend of mine who really wants something you have."

Before Millie could answer, she and Crackers felt a chill sweep under the door and right across them.

"Millie, the real girl – I've been waiting for this moment for a very long time. Ever since you first tweeted in Titter that you were in possession of a magic Zablet. I've been watching you across all of your adventures. Your pictures … your updates … so interesting. And now I have you where I want you."

"I'm a real girl too," chipped in Ethel.

"Shut up! Can't you see I'm busy?" said the witch, then turned back to the door.

"Who are you?" gasped Millie. "And what do you want with us?"

The witch screeched with wicked laughter. "You?" she howled. "You?! I don't want anything with you. Or the little scruff, for that matter. I want the Zablet. Your Zablet. The most powerful enchanted Zablet in all of the human world. A portal between the magical cyber-world and the real world. It must be mine."

Changing the subject, the witch then said, "However, this little brat next to me wants to ensure you are forever trapped in this world. It seems a small price to pay."

Millie cried out, "Ethel, this is going too far! You've been bullying here, there and everywhere for too long!"

172

"I'm a bully. It's what I do," said Ethel with a smirk.

"Let's get on with this," cackled the witch. "I need to cast a return spell on myself instead of on the Millie girl. The Zablet will take *me* back into the real world instead, where I can take control of it."

A wicked smile crept across her lips. "I may even have some fun when I get there."

Millie was horrified. She knew Harry had the Zablet. If a witch leapt out of it he would be terrified, and who knew what she would do to him? Millie couldn't bear to think of it.

She turned to Crackers again. "Oh, Crackers, what will we do?"

Crackers replied tearfully, "I don't know, Mills. I just don't know."

Madam Twinkle tiptoed down the staircase and then along the dimly lit passageway. She could hear voices up ahead. Millie and Crackers! They sounded very upset.

And that other horrid, sickening, cackling voice must be the witch.

As Madam Twinkle peered around the corner she saw the witch raise her wand and begin to chant the words of a spell, one she recognised as a return spell. She had to act right away.

Madam Twinkle hurled Teddy Bear at the witch, and as he arced through the air he began to scatter the spell mixture over her!

The witch turned to see what was happening, and Madam Twinkle began to chant her own spell. She had to get her words out more quickly than the witch could.

Fortunately Madam Twinkle's banishment spell was much shorter.

Banish!

Vanish!

Witch begone!

The witch faced Madam Twinkle, enraged and covered in dust and goo.

Millie and Crackers could hear the commotion on the other side of the door.

"What's going on, Crackers?" shouted Millie.

"I don't know for sure –" he sounded hopeful – "but it sounds as if Madam Twinkle is back."

"Noooooooo!" shrieked the witch, but it was too late. She began to fade and shrink all at the same time.

Ethel had seen enough and set off back down the corridor, but as she ran past him Teddy Bear bravely threw himself at her feet and she tripped and fell to the floor.

The witch had gone. The banishment spell had worked beautifully.

"Now your turn, you spiteful, horrid little bully," said Madam Twinkle as she turned on the fallen Ethel and poured more of the mixture on her.

Banish!

Vanish!

You horrid girl!

You won't be missed!

Ethel writhed and struggled but it was no use; she too shrank and faded until she had completely disappeared.

Millie and Crackers heard the jangling of keys and the dungeon door swung open.

A beaming Madam Twinkle greeted them with arms flung wide.

They were free!

Madam Twinkle explained to them what had happened and how clever and brave Teddy had been. He really had been a hero too and looked ever so pleased as Millie and Crackers picked him up and hugged him.

As they walked back to the shop Madam Twinkle spoke to Millie. "I think it's time for you to go home now too, Millie."

Millie looked worried. "But, Madam Twinkle, Ethel's back there – she'll be waiting for me at school. This will just carry on. Can't you help me and stop her bullying in the real world too?"

Madam Twinkle stopped and looked kindly at Millie, but she shook her head. "No, I can't. I can only help you in cyberspace, but I know it doesn't stop here, Millie. I can kick bullies out of this world for you, but in the real world the only way you can stop her bullying is by telling a real grown-up. That means your mother and father or even a teacher. You must tell them about it. Promise me you will tell someone, Millie," she insisted.

Millie sighed. She didn't want to worry her parents or admit she was being bullied.

"But before I send you back," said Madam Twinkle with a glint in her eye, "let's have some fun."

And what fun they had. Madam Twinkle took them back to the shop and showed them her own recipe for ice cream. Far from making you big, it could make you whatever you wanted if you just wished it before you ate it. Tiny, round, thin, flat and Millie's personal favourite, invisible.

Crackers wanted to see what it would be like to be big, and Madam Twinkle made sure he went outside first so as not to crash through the ceiling of her shop. It was also important they made up a batch of the zip-up spell dust beforehand.

Next they rode on fireworks around FaceSpace, which was exciting and terrifying! They sat on big rockets as Teddy Bear lit the fuse and off they flew, whizzing over houses and gardens, up into the clouds and, as the sparks fizzled out and they came plummeting back to earth, Madam Twinkle was there to make sure they landed safely on enormous bouncy castles that had appeared from nowhere!

Finally Madam Twinkle took them back inside the shop and through another tiny door into a room so large it seemed impossible – the shop was so tiny from the outside!

A huge dining table stretched from one end of the room to the other. Madam Twinkle clicked her fingers and the candlesticks lit themselves and started humming a lovely song, the cutlery jumped out of boxes and the plates rolled themselves to places at the table where cards were with the names MILLIE, CRACKERS, MADAM TWINKLE, TEDDY BEAR.

Madam Twinkle clapped her hands and all manner of food appeared before them. Roast chicken, succulent vegetables, pizza, pasta, warm crusty bread, cheese, fruit, crisps, cakes and ice cream, there really was no end. It was an amazing feast.

When they had feasted until they were as full as they had ever been, Millie sighed contentedly and said to the others, "I feel as if I've eaten so much I'm as big as when I ate that BIS ice cream."

They all laughed, but Madam Twinkle assured her that wasn't the case.

Finally Madam Twinkle rose and raised her glass. "A toast!" she declared.

"To Millie – our newest member of cyberspace and one of the bravest we have ever known. To Millie!"

They all raised their glasses. Crackers leaned across to Millie and whispered to her, "You need to be brave in your world now, Mills."

Millie knew it was true, and when Madam Twinkle stood up again and said, "It's time for you to go back now, Millie," she knew she was ready.

THE END

The Magic Zablet was written as a means of educating children (and adults too!) about some of the perils and pitfalls that they might encounter when using the Internet, or – as is now becoming the common term – cyberspace.

The book is intended to be fun to read, while identifying the dangers and consequently the behaviours that will help guard against those threats; by embedding it all within a story.

However, following extensive discussions with my editorial team (OK, my wife and daughters) I thought it would be beneficial to include an accompanying guide which a parent (or other reader) might use to flag particular issues as they are being addressed.

Why not review this section with your children after each chapter and ask them if they felt they learned anything that they should remember when using the Internet?

Chapter 1

This chapter introduces the central characters, but the lesson to take away is that there should be an uncertainty of who people really are in the cyber-world. The Tyler family had no idea who Madam Twinkle really was.

Chapter 2

This is about Millie getting to grips with her new Zablet, learning about the apps and its appeal.

Chapter 3

This is where the learning curve really begins. The land of Titter is based on a very popular social-networking site and is intended to highlight the following:

- Things you say can be repeated and echoed again and again, making the impact worse than you intended as more and more people hear (or read) them.
- Saying something you don't really mean can land you in a lot of trouble.
- Things said in the cyber-world can be hurtful and spiteful, just as in the real world.

Chapters 4, 5 and 6

Those shouting the loudest with the most followers are listened to and believed.

- Trolls – In the cyber-world, just as in the real world it's very difficult to tell who bad people are.
- These chapters also reinforce the point of being careful and mindful about what you say in the cyber-world, as it can

come back to haunt you. It won't disappear just because you didn't mean it or have changed your mind.

Chapters 7 and 8

The relationship with Ethel takes a more sinister turn here as it becomes evident she is bullying Millie.

Millie uses the Zablet to escape to a place that is nicer than the real world which has Ethel in it.

Chapter 9

This is mainly bringing the Mesalonia story to a finish but does introduce the concept of deleting data and it being gone forever.

Chapter 10

When something seems too good to be true, it probably is.

Millie accepted an offer that really was unlikely to be true.

Chapter 11

Once Millie was infected, the "virus" spread to Harry.

Chapter 12

Pictures are taken all the time, creating a record in cyberspace of everything you do.

Chapter 13

Be conscious of what pictures of you are put online. This is about your privacy.

- Once in cyberspace, the pictures are there forever, creating your digital identity and footprint.
- Things you do in one world or country might be judged differently in another. Look at the barmy judge's loony law on clowns and all of the other people he convicted.
- Pictures can also be deleted from immediate view.

Chapter 14

Personal information matched with a fingerprint could be used against you. Theo realised this and made a plan to jumble up their details.

Chapter 15

Millie left her device unlocked so anyone could pick it up and use it.

- Others might want to look around your tablet/Zablet, devices and online profile.
- Teaches an awareness of how pictures online could advertise that you weren't where you were supposed to be (when Gavin realises they should have been in school for instance).
- Gavin considered abusing the trust the other children had put in him and accessing Millie's Zablet for his own curiosity.

Chapter 16

Geolocation added to pictures makes you easier to find. It's how the children were found in InstaPic.

People take pictures of everything and put them online!

Chapters 17, 18 and 19

- Online bullying. Ethel gave Millie's details away to hurt her.
- The nature of personal details – the pirates' treasure is the personal details of their captives. How will they use them to plunder and steal?
- Hackers – did Hooky "hack" into Millie's Zablet in order to pull her in? The pirates were going to hack into the online accounts of their captives in order to steal.
- What happens to your details if they are stolen? How are they used by criminals?
- The true identity of online "friends" – Hooky wasn't who he seemed, was he?
- Avatars – Millie's picture was of an ice princess, but she wasn't one in real life.
- Offers too good to be true. All of the pirates' captives complain about how they were tricked with promises of things that were too good to be true.
- If you have a problem, you need to ask for help. The police can help.
- Tell a grown-up if you are being bullied, online or in the real world.

Chapter 20

Bullying. Millie again finds escape in the Zablet.

Chapters 21 and 22

How Facebook and other such sites work. The concept is introduced through analogies of a busy city, houses (pads), etc.

- Do you really want to be "friends" with everyone?
- Things are not always what they seem. Such as the BIG I SCREAM man. He tricked Millie.
- Trust. Whom do you really trust?

Chapters 23 to 29

- Verifying identities. In the Be-Who-You-Want port anybody could take on any identity they wished for.
- Passwords. Ethel gained access to Millie's FaceSpace app by guessing her password as Millie had chosen one that was easy to guess.
- Passwords. The witch left her password in places they could be easily found.
- People's intent. Why did the BIG I SCREAM man give Millie the ice cream?

Chapters 30, 31 and 32

Bullying – online and in the real world. Ethel followed Millie into cyberspace so she could continue the bullying. Does Millie have any escape from Ethel's bullying?

Millie's friends reinforce the point that she must tell a grown-up about Ethel's bullying.

ABOUT THE AUTHOR AND THE BOOK

Having worked in computer security for over fifteen years I've listened to and read much regarding the commonly held belief that people are the weakest link.

Hundreds of thousands, if not millions, of dollars and pounds are spent on state-of-the-art technologies designed to protect our computer systems, but these defences are often rendered useless when the human being is tricked or lured into doing something they shouldn't.

But how do they know they shouldn't have done what it is they did?

Many cybersecurity industry leaders are now looking at behavioural and cognitive psychology as a means of understanding why humans continue to adopt the role of the weakest link.

In addition, neuroscience demonstrates how neural pathways are formed in our brains that dictate decisions that we make and the way we behave in certain situations. These pathways are formed through experiences and new things we learn.

Many of the next generation of Internet users are currently five to ten years old. This generation is going to be absolutely embedded within a cyber-world, completely surrounded by Internet-connected devices in the home, at school, at work and everywhere else. It will be a way of life.

As the father of two wonderful girls, the eldest of whom falls into that age group and the other who will fairly shortly, I decided to fuse together two of the things I spend the most time doing and which are therefore my areas of expertise: computer security and reading children's books. I wanted to write a book that was fun and enjoyable to read, but which called out behaviours and lessons that the target audience might be able to take with them into this future cyber-world.

I set out with an aim for the book to be half fantasy/fiction and half about cybersecurity. If I'm honest, I think the end result is more of the former as I had too much fun writing it, but that's OK; there are already guides and training available out there, and education in general seems to be slowly developing its capability and strategies to teach this generation about computer security. But I believe children – and people in general – truly absorb lessons and learn best when they are thoroughly enjoying what they are doing. Therefore I hope children who read *The Magic Zablet*, either with or without their parents, enjoy it and, if they take just one lesson from it, just one thing that might make them think twice in a hazardous situation when using a computer; then it was worth it.

James.

More information

Email: Crackers@Gosnold.Co.Uk

Web: www.magiczablet.com

Twitter: @TheMagicZablet

22388675R00118

Printed in Great Britain
by Amazon